CW00734291

SOUTH WALES VALLEYS

Edward A. Evans

CONTENTS

INTRODUCTION

When the commissioning editor approached me with the idea of producing this book, I wondered at first what I should include between the covers that would be of interest to those who cared to read it. But to begin with, I think it only proper that I should let the reader know that I am not an expert and have never professed to be. Apart from a general enthusiasm for the railways of south east Wales, it is the work of railwaymen which is my premier area of interest.

For instance, when travelling by train to school in the 1950s, it was commonplace to see a man patrolling the lineside armed with what appeared to be a long-handled hammer. The man, of course, used it to drive home a loosened oak key. This I easily understood was part of his daily duty as a patrolman. But, I often thought, what does he really do? What problems did he encounter? I had the same thoughts concerning the work of a shunter. I knew he spent a good deal of his time, armed with a hooked pole, making up trains in a definite order.

But, again, what did a shunter's job really entail? One of the chapters in this book will give an insight into such a man's work in a big yard north of Cardiff.

Ever since I can remember, railways have held a fascination for me and I maintain that the 1950s — and this is an opinion with which I do not expect everyone to agree — was the most interesting decade in the history of Britain's railways. But even then the subject did not receive my fullest attention as it was one amongst four major pastimes. Two visits a week to the local cinema were an accepted way of life in those days as were the two seasons of the year, soccer and cricket. That said, I believe all four pastimes received equal enthusiasm.

I have never had the slightest interest in Acts of Parliament or the politics of railways. These subjects, I find, are best left to those experienced authors who have produced excellent work; they can be rightly described as experts or authorities and who spend hours at the Public Records Office patiently unravelling historical data. Nor did I stand at the end of a

Nelson and Llancaiach was the starting point from which the author and his colleagues made frequent journeys on many of the local lines in the late 1950s. In this view, looking towards Hengoed, GWR '56XX' Class 0-6-2T No.5624 pauses at the down platform with the 6.15p.m. Cardiff—Aberdare (High Level) train on 15th July 1959. The station was brought into use by the GWR on 1st July 1912 as a replacement for Llancaiach which was Nelson's *first station and which had served the public for 54 years. The outer face of the island platform on the far left was used by passenger traffic to and from Dowlais (Cae Harris). It will be noted that the platforms were embellished by shrubs and flower beds; these attractive features, for which many prizes were won, were established by porter William (Bill) Cooper who was the last man to be employed at the station. (HCC/RMC)*

Deserted platforms and passengers no more on a high summer day in August 1964 at Nelson and Llancaiach. But freight continued and two months after withdrawal of the passenger service between Neath and Pontypool Road, an unidentified GWR '56XX' Class 0-6-2T trundles eastwards through the station with a load of coal from Ocean and Taff Merthyr. (R. H. Marrows)

platform with a notebook and pencil recording the names and numbers of passing engines. I did not have an Ian Allan ABC; in fact, the first I ever possessed was bought in a charity shop a few years ago.

But I did enjoy sitting on a platform bench at our station watching coal trains trundling eastwards and observing the variety of motive power that could be seen at work on the Vale of Neath. Another enjoyable pastime was travelling by railway just to see where a line went and, perhaps, why it had been put there in the first place. I had a few friends of the same age who usually accompanied me. Together, we travelled to such places as Aberdare, Pontypool Road, Merthyr, Cardiff and Barry Island. This was in the happier, slower world of the mid-1950s when twelve and thirteen-year-olds could travel in complete safety.

Once, we decided to book half returns to Dowlais (Cae Harris). One of my friends had discovered that the old steel town was riddled with railway stations and that it would be a grand idea to try and visit them all. We didn't: the next train to

take us home was due for departure in an hour. But we did see Dowlais (High Street), which was a stone's throw from Cae Harris. We clambered up the steep path to the platform only to be disappointed. There was not a living soul in sight. The station appeared as if it were sleeping. More than that, the station was dying. This was confirmed by a tall, angular, smiling porter who, at snail's pace, emerged from his ticket office to empty the dregs of his brown china teapot over the platform edge. The station, he said, before returning to his inner sanctum for yet another forty winks, was due for closure in a few weeks' time.

Locally and in railway terms, Abercynon was a place which held a special attraction because it had an engine shed. And although it was not on our line, we could reach it in an hour provided we walked briskly enough along the banks of the coal-stained River Taff. Our first visit was on a warm, sunny Saturday afternoon. There was very little activity but a young engine cleaner made our day by inviting us over the footbridge to see his place of work. To this day I believe the youngster was glad to have someone to talk to.

Signalmen, however, weren't so obliging and pointed to the cast iron warning notice on the box door whenever an approach was made to have a look inside at the world of bakelite telephones, block bells, levers and polished linoleum. But one 'bobby' could see that we were genuinely interested and invited us to sit on the wooden bench at the back of his box. He gave us a stern warning that if a train stopped at the platform we were to keep our heads down and not be seen by

The Monmouthshire Railway Society's 'Rambling 56', en route to Dowlais (Cae Harris), pauses at Nelson & Llancaiach on 31st July 1965. Note that the bi-directional branch platform line has been lifted and much of the signalling equipment has been recovered. (R. H. Marrows)

anyone in authority. It was during subsequent visits to the signal box, I was reminded that men made railways work and from that time on I developed a particular interest in the jobs undertaken by railwaymen.

When I started work in 1961 I was naïve. I believed the railway that then existed and I had grown up with would go on forever. It would always be there and nothing would change. A few years later it passed me by that there was a man lurking in the shadows about to wield a big axe which would cut the branches from Britain's railway tree. I had taken it all for granted and at that time my interest in railways had waned. It was also a period of personal regret because I did not take the trouble to travel on the Newport to Brecon line of the old Brecon & Merthyr. I could have done it, but somehow I didn't and by the end of 1962 the passenger service had gone. It is too late now but perhaps one day some bright spark will invent a magic carpet so that I can travel, in the comfort of a Western Region railway carriage, through the curving tunnel at Torpantau and experience the delight of descending the seven-mile bank to Talybont.

One morning in 1968, when I was due to work an afternoon shift, I killed an hour by wandering down to our station which had been chopped by the man with the big axe four years earlier. The station itself was intact and the signal box was still

in use for coal traffic to Ocean & Taff Merthyr and for coal and foundry traffic to Dowlais. The track layout had been heavily rationalised and much of the signalling equipment had been recovered. One man, porter William Cooper, was still employed there, supervising traffic into and out of the goods yard which had become a coal depot. It was during half an hour's conversation with Mr. Cooper, who was nearing retirement, I realised what had gone. Following the chance meeting, my interest in railways was rekindled. For Christmas 1969 my wife bought me Ian Krause's *Great Western Branch Line Album*, which featured many of the South Wales lines upon which I had travelled. The publication is an Ian Allan gem. If I were asked, this is the book I would want with me on a desert island. It is also a nostalgic little book because it reminded me in the late 1960s what had been lost forever.

When planning this book I had difficulty in settling on a theme. I decided, therefore, in a couple of cases, to update a few articles which had appeared in a railway magazine some time ago. Then I chose to add a few original pen pictures of locations with which I had experience or a general knowledge. My interest in the jobs railwaymen did is also reflected in these pages for without such men of varied skills railways cannot work. I have relied heavily on the recollections of retired and currently active railwaymen in the hope that a personal picture in words and photographs will be given of the valleys of south east Wales.

Edward A. Evans
Nelson, Glamorgan
December 2004

A GWR Survivor in the Valleys

Signalling ancient and modern at Abercynon

It was in 1995, during the research for a short article on the signal box at Abercynon which was published in a now defunct monthly railway magazine, that I was required to apply for permission to the relevant authorities to be allowed an official visit to the box. Permission was granted and an appointment was made to view the box in the company of the Railtrack signalling manager, Cardiff.

I was not disappointed. The interior of the box was in immaculate condition; the equipment on the block shelf sparkled and the linoleum floor covering was spotless. The proverbial duster hung from a facing point lock lever that stood in the locked position. I thought at the time that I was fortunate to be shown a survivor from another age.

The railway scene at Abercynon is much changed from the

Signalling equipment ancient and modern in Abercynon signal box, 18th August 1995. The kitchen area can be seen beyond the partition at the south end of the box. At the far end of the operating floor is the colour light signal and point/switch indicator panel which controlled Stormstown yard. In the centre is the 34-lever frame which was shortened in 1971. To the right of the frame is the Tyer's single line instrument for the Merthyr line. The GEC SSI Mini Panel (Aberdare line) is to the right. For students of signalling it will be noted that the single line token has been returned to the instrument. This, together with the positions of the levers, confirms that a down Merthyr—Cardiff train has just passed the box. Resident signalman Mr. Norman Kingston is 'on the blower'. The train register can be seen on the desk to his right. (Author)

Abercynon signal box as it appeared on 17th August 1986. It was during the 1980s that the box was bricked up to operating floor level. In the early 1990s the roof was renewed and the traditional GWR vents removed. The door and steps were added in the early 1970s to facilitate speedier access to the platform for the signalman. Trains on the Merthyr line stop twice at Abercynon, once to drop off or pick up passengers at the north end of the platform, and again at the box when the token is surrendered or accepted. S&T Department buildings can be seen on the extreme left. The Aberdare branch is to the right. (Author)

bustling junction I knew in the late 1950s. I recall the Aberdare auto trains sprinting out of the platform and around the curve to Pontcynon and an ex-GWR '56XX' Class 0-6-2T working hard and wheezing as it tackled the big bank to Quaker's Yard with six coaches in tow. And there was yard activity outside the shed. One feature that stands out in my memory is what was called the 'van road' on which stood a line of 20-ton brake vans, better known as 'Toads'.

Today, the big, draughty island platform is characterless and unnecessarily long for the two-car Sprinters and Pacers that run to Merthyr and Cardiff at regular intervals. The station buildings and the platform canopy which provided shelter were demolished over three decades ago. Only the up side is in use these days and where once were welcoming, comfortable, coal-heated waiting and ladies' rooms, there is a forgettable, austere brick-built shelter.

Abercynon's saving grace is that it is still of interest to students of signalling. It is one of three locations where semaphore signalling survives on the valley lines running north from Cardiff; the others are at Ystrad Mynach and Bargoed on the Rhymney line. There is added interest at Abercynon in that alongside the mechanical lever frame stands the technology of a new age in the form of a mini panel which was installed following the reinstatement of passenger services to Aberdare in the late 1980s.

But more on the signal box itself a little later as here it may be useful to pause and say something of Abercynon as a railway junction. It has a long history on the railway map of south east Wales, being an original station on the Taff Vale Railway's main line from Cardiff to Merthyr which was opened throughout in 1841. Above the station was the 1 in 11 rope-worked main incline which Brunel, engineer to the TVR,

ABERCYNON

AS AT 1995
DIAGRAMMATIC ONLY

TO YNYSYBWL (Out of use)

TO PONTYPRIDD

UP

DOWN   MAIN

DOWN   BRANCH   UP

DOWN   MAIN   UP

ABERCYNON NORTH

TO ABERDARE

TO MERTHYR

SAND DRAG

ABERCYNON SOUTH

favoured as a means of surmounting a steep rise in terrain towards Quaker's Yard. The incline was replaced in 1867 by an easier locomotive deviation even though its gradient was still formidably steep at 1 in 38 and 1 in 42.

The original main incline and the replacement locomotive deviation were prominent features of the Abercynon landscape. A few yards to the west was another, even more impressive engineering achievement. This was Thomas Dadford's 'Abercynon Sixteen', a staircase of locks which lowered the Glamorganshire Canal from the foothills of Cefn Glas down to Abercynon. This engineering masterpiece was completed in 1791 and predated the opening of the TVR main incline by half a century.

The station and junction has rejoiced at various times during its history under three different names. In its earliest days it was known as Navigation House. In 1846 the Aberdare branch was opened but it took another four years for the TVR to rename the station to Aberdare Junction.

In 1893 the residents of the mining village held a meeting in the infants' school in an attempt to decide finally on a name for their settlement. It had been known at various times as 'Navigation', 'The Basin' (after the nearby Glamorganshire Canal), the tongue-twisting 'Ynysfeirig' and the more straightforward 'Aberdare Junction'. The residents, it would appear, wanted something simple rather than 'Abertafachynon', which was one of the proposals put forward. The rather attractive 'Cynonvale' was suggested but the meeting finally decided upon 'Abercynon' which means mouth of the Cynon (river). With the populace finally reaching agreement, the TVR duly renamed the station 'Abercynon' on 1st December 1896.

The early station had been resited in 1848 and consisted of an island platform. By 1897 a new booking office and an overall canopy had been provided and the platforms lengthened. The station remained in this state until the demolition of the buildings and the rationalisation of the track layout in the early 1970s.

The first engine shed at Abercynon was brought into use by the TVR in 1853. This shed was replaced in 1929 by a larger two-road shed. In 1926 nineteen locomotives were allocated to Abercynon. By 1947 the allocation had risen to 28, consisting of 0-6-0PTs, ten of Collett's '56XX' Class 0-6-2Ts and a few aged ex-TVR 0-6-2 tanks. Most of the locomotives were employed on coal traffic, shunting at Stormstown, and banking duties to Quaker's Yard. Abercynon also provided the motive power for passenger turns to Aberdare, Merthyr and to Ynysybwl. An auto-fitted '64XX' Class 0-6-0PT worked the Pontypridd—Caerphilly—Machen service. The shed closed in November 1964.

Abercynon had a signal box at both ends of the station. Abercynon South (44 levers), which stood on the up side, was opened in about 1886. South was closed in 1908 and replaced by a new box containing 64 levers. The opening date of Abercynon North is not known but it was equipped with 45 levers. In 1897 it was replaced by a new box with 60 levers.

Early in 1932 a burst main sewer damaged Abercynon South box. The extent of the damage was considerable, so much so that the GWR decided that it was not worth carrying out repairs. Both South and North boxes were taken out of use, replaced by a new, bigger, box of timber construction and with a hipped roof at the south end of the island platform and as such the signalling at Abercynon was centralised. However, the box was not brand-new for the structure had stood in two other locations far from the Welsh valleys. It had begun its working life at Birmingham Moor Street where it was in use from 27th June 1909 until 7th September 1913. Then it was moved to Foxhall Junction, Didcot, opening on 27th November 1915 and closing on 31st October 1931. At Abercynon it was brought into operation on 10th April 1932. Over 70 years later it is still in use and adds a little sparkle to relieve the dullness that is today's Abercynon station.

At the time of my officially-sanctioned visit to Abercynon box, Mr. Norman Kingston, one of three resident signalmen, happened to be on duty. Over a period of about three hours Mr. Kingston patiently explained the workings of the box which turned out to be a veritable Aladdin's Cave of systems ancient and modern. It had originally been equipped with a GWR vertical tappet, five-bar 93-lever frame to control what was a large and complicated layout which included a scissors crossover south of the box, but with the rationalisation of 1971 the frame had been shortened to 34 levers. During its heyday the box was interfaced with Quaker's Yard (Low Level) to the north on the Merthyr line and Carn Parc to the south. On the Aberdare line it made communication with Pontcynon Junction. By the mid-1960s these boxes had closed which meant that up until 1977 it was interfaced with Stormstown Junction to the south where there was a yard and where a single line wandered off to the north west to Lady Windsor Colliery, Ynysybwl. The box also controlled the entrance to Abercynon Colliery.

Following the closure of Stormstown Junction box, control of the yard, traffic into Abercynon colliery and on the branch to Windsor Colliery was passed to Abercynon. Stormstown yard was worked by means of a switch panel which was positioned to the left of the mechanical frame. All new connections at the yard were worked by electro-hydraulic clamp lock-type machines. The train staff for working the line to Lady Windsor Colliery was kept in a key release instrument

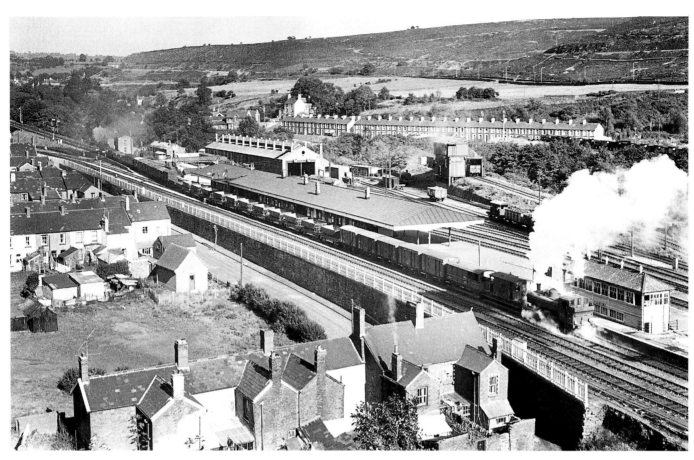

housed in a hut and was released from Abercynon box. The yard was equipped with loud-sounding bells when the Abercynon signalman needed to contact shunters and other personnel. The former block sections Pontypridd—Stormstown—Abercynon were replaced by track circuit block, Pontypridd—Abercynon.

To control the yard a colour light and point indicator panel was installed in the box. It was designed by the S&T Department's Chief Installer and Tester. Signalman Kingston informed me that it was a reliable piece of equipment and, owing to its appearance, adorned as it was with circular dials, was humorously referred to as 'Arthur Salter's Olympic Scoreboard'.

In 1971 the line to Merthyr was singled north of Abercynon with a passing place retained at Black Lion, near Merthyr Vale. The line was worked by Tyer's single line token as was, at the time, the freight-only line to Aberdare. Both token instruments stood side by side to the right of the frame.

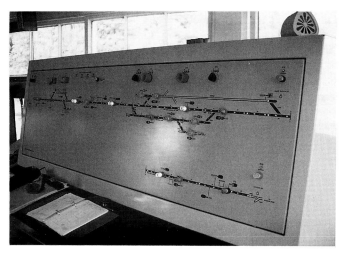

The SSI mini panel, Abercynon, August 1995. (Author)

The changing face of Abercynon. A period of 27 years separates these two views of the station and it is interesting to spot the differences. In the upper picture an unidentified GWR 0-6-0PT is providing spirited assistance as it banks a freight on the Merthyr line on 23rd September 1964. Abercynon signal box can be seen in its original all-timber form with the entrance at the south end. The station canopy is clearly shown on the island platform. In the middle background is the shed with a GWR '56XX' Class 0-6-2T near the coaling stage. The shed closed two months later. The far right background shows the alignment of the original TVR Llancaiach branch of 1841 following a contour of Graig Evan Leyshon and can be traced to St. Cynon's on the extreme left. At a lower level the later deviation, upon which the Nelson branch passenger trains ran, is marked by the lamp standards on the Merthyr—Cardiff road.

The lower picture was taken from the same vantage point on 18th April 1991. An unidentified Class 37 is about to come off the Aberdare branch with a train of mgr hopper wagons from Tower Colliery to Aberthaw power station. Note that by this time the entrance to the signal box is by means of steps at the north end and the building has been bricked-up to operating floor level. The engine shed still stands but has been refurbished for private use. The line running behind the platform is the former down line which is in use as a sand drag; the safety points on the Merthyr line can be seen top left, to the left of the station house. Public access to the platform is by means of a subway, the entrance to which can be seen in the street below the tenth hopper from the end of the train. (Both photographs by B. J. Ashworth)

In the mid-1980s Christmas shopping excursions and mystery trips were run from Aberdare on selected weekends, these trains proving popular with the people of the Aberdare Valley who had lost their passenger service in 1964. The success of these trains prompted Mid-Glamorgan County Council to investigate the possible re-introduction of a regular passenger service to Aberdare after a break of almost a quarter of a century.

In October 1988 the passenger service was reinstated on the Aberdare line. A year later, on 9th October, a new GEC Solid State Interlocking Mini Panel was installed in Abercynon box, using track circuit block and thus bringing the entire line to Aberdare under the supervision of the Abercynon signalman. Semaphore signalling controlled the station area and the modern mini panel the line to Aberdare. With the demise of Stormstown yard, 'Salter's Olympic Scoreboard' sees little use.

Once beyond the semaphore starter at Abercynon North, the progress of an Aberdare-bound train along the single line can be followed. On the panel a series of closely-spaced green lamps highlights the route, so the signalman is aware at all times of the train's position. A train's passage past a signal causes the aspect to change to danger automatically and the green route lamps on the panel to go out on that part of the line which has been traversed. Whilst the train stands at the Aberdare terminus, the signalman resets the route, using illuminated push-buttons, for the return journey. The mini panel is equipped with an axle counter.

Beyond Aberdare the single line to Tower Colliery, Hirwaun, is freight only worked 'One Train Only' with an occupation token. Between Aberdare and Hirwaun there are two level crossings and these are 'Train Man Operated'.

With the introduction of the passenger service to Aberdare, a problem had arisen in that as the Merthyr traffic in both

Abercynon signal box in its original form, September 1967. Note how the box has been lowered into a pit excavated at the end of the island platform. This was necessary to give the signalmen a reasonable view up the line beneath the platform canopy. It is useful to compare this photograph with the later examples to appreciate the various changes in the box's appearance. (R. H. Marrows)

directions used one side of the island platform, extensive track and signalling alterations would have to have been made to accommodate the trains that would run to and from Aberdare. This would have been expensive work but a solution was achieved by opening a new station, named Abercynon North, on the Aberdare line. The old station was, logically, renamed Abercynon South.

The mini panel, which stands to the right of the frame, was soon discovered to be a sensitive piece of equipment. Its occasional bad state of health was caused by heat and dust from the Romesse coal stove. The stove was removed from the box and heating was later provided by a wall-mounted electric fire and a couple of convector heaters.

Unlike signal boxes in the early days of railways, and in fact during comparatively recent years, when the signalman's personal needs were given scant consideration, Abercynon signal box in modern times can be reasonably described as home from home. At the south end, where steps lead down to the locking room, a partitioned area has been set aside as a kitchen. A refrigerator, hot and cold running water, an electric cooker and a microwave oven have been provided.

Tyer's No. 7 single line electric train token instrument for the Merthyr line, August 1995. (Author)

The box has been renovated a number of times in recent years. In the mid-1980s it was bricked up as far as operating floor lever. It has received a new roof which appears to have been renewed using composite slates. The entrance to the box was originally at the south end but in 1971 steps were provided at the north end which made it easier and quicker for the signalman to reach the platform to issue or receive the single line token from the driver of a train on the Merthyr line.

The box has three windows in the back wall. This is a reminder of days gone by when both sides of the island platform were in use and when the signalman needed to have a clear view of down traffic and a waiting engine at the shed yard signal. One of the original GWR cast iron nameplates — there was one on either side of the box — was rescued by one of the resident signalmen. A general factotum had been sent to replace it with a bland tin version but signalman Morris must have had a sense of history when he rescued the cast iron plate and had it bolted to the back wall of the box.

Abercynon is the last mechanical signal box on the former Taff Vale main line. The others at Llandaff Loop, Radyr Junction, Walnut Tree, Maesmawr and Pontypridd closed in the late 1990s when control of the line as far north as Abercynon, and the line to Treherbert in Rhondda Fawr, passed to the new signalling centre at Radyr.

Over the past decade there have been rumours as to the future of Abercynon signal box, especially when one bears in mind the number of boxes made redundant by the new signalling scheme that was put in place in the late 1990s.

Light and shade inside Abercynon shed, October 1963. GWR '56XX' Class 0-6-2T No. 5699 is the only identifiable engine of the five on view. (R. H. Marrows)

Abercynon could have gone the same way. Thankfully it has survived to remind the railway historian that there is still a relic of the old railway on the former TVR main line.

Abercynon shed closed to steam at the end of 1964 but for a few years was retained as a signing-on point, train crews using a room on the island platform. In this September 1967 view, taken from the down side, half a dozen Class 37 diesels are seen standing in the yard, with two brake vans in the van road. In the background, to the left of the shed, can be seen the station house and the staff canteen. (R. H. Marrows)

2

The Penalltau Branch

An account of a short branch which connected the Rhymney Railway with the GWR

The Rhymney Railway (RR) had interests in a couple of joint lines remote from its Cardiff—Rhymney main line. The first, the Taff Bargoed Joint, a partnership with the Great Western Railway, ran from Llancaiach to Dowlais and was brought into use in 1876 for both passenger and freight traffic. Vast quantities of iron ore were dragged up the fearsome gradients of this double line to Dowlais Works.

The second line, remote from the RR's main line, was the Quaker's Yard & Merthyr Joint, again an alliance with the GWR. Opened for traffic in 1886, it ran from Quaker's Yard to Merthyr, via Aberfan, on the western side of the Taff Valley. The opening of its Penalltau branch gave the RR access to the Vale of Neath over which it had running powers to Hirwaun. Later, the branch also acted as a 'gateway' to the two joint lines.

The branch was one and a half miles in length and left the RR main line at Ystrad Junction to ascend on a gradient of 1 in 84 to Penalltau Junction on the GWR's Vale of Neath line. This junction was situated between Rhymney Junction (later Hengoed) and Llancaiach. At opening the branch was single but, owing to an increase in traffic, was doubled by 1900. There was a change of direction at Penalltau Junction, the up line of the branch trailing into the down line of the Vale of Neath.

Construction of the branch was relatively straightforward. Two bridges were required: the first was a rail overbridge at Brynmynach where the lower end of the branch crossed the Nelson—Ystrad Mynach road which was once a turnpike road. The second was a rail underbridge at the upper end where the branch, as it climbed towards the junction, began to run parallel with the Vale of Neath. This was at a place called Pencarth where an area of rock had to be excavated and a bridge constructed to provide access to some early Penalltau Colliery Sidings.

The branch was opened for traffic on 1st April 1871. Ystrad Junction signal box, on the RR's main line, controlled the entrance to the branch at its lower end (Penalltau Branch Junction). The box was brought into use at the opening of the branch but was renamed Ystrad South to distinguish it from Ystrad North which stood half a mile to the north on the main line. Ystrad South was closed in 1886, replaced by the dressed-stone McKenzie & Holland box which is still in use

today. By this time it carried the name Ystrad Mynach South. The lever frame was extended in about 1899 no doubt in preparation for the doubling of the Penalltau branch. In 1938 it was equipped with a 46-lever standard GWR vertical tappet frame.

The box stood on an embankment on the up side, where the main line curved its way towards Ystrad Mynach station. From the operating floor, the signalman was afforded a fine view of the main line in both directions, the junction for the branch and the entrance to the exchange sidings on the down side. Owing to its elevated position of about fifteen feet above rail level, signal wires and point rodding ran, with the assistance of pulleys, down the embankment, where at track level another group of pulleys and cranks sent wire and rodding in the required directions.

Surprisingly and considering the age of the box, the 'crank platform', which now carries the wires and rodding in more orderly fashion down to rail level, is a comparatively recent addition, being added to the box some time in the 1950s. The actual date has been difficult to pin down.

For a signal box that has been in use for over a century, there is a story, related to me by a signalman once employed at the box, that adds a little interest to the history of the place. I was informed that during 1945, electrical wiring which ran round the fireplace became faulty and caused a fire. Damage to paintwork and to signalling equipment was by no means slight. But worst of all was the destruction of the roof. However, traffic still had to run and for a time the signalmen at Ystrad Mynach South, without the benefit of a good dry roof, were required to work in raincoats during inclement weather. It is not known how long it took to provide the new roof.

In 1988 signalman Lewis showed me a Bible that had been kept in the box for many years and had been signed by some of the signalmen who had been employed there. The Bible was presented to the box late in the nineteenth century by the Cardiff Railway Mission.

Here it is interesting to note that in 2001 signalman Mr. Maurice Jones retired. He had been resident signalman at Ystrad Mynach South for 40 years. Surely this must be some kind of record for the length of uninterrupted service by one man in one signal box!

THE PENALLTAU BRANCH

SHOWING CONNECTING LINES

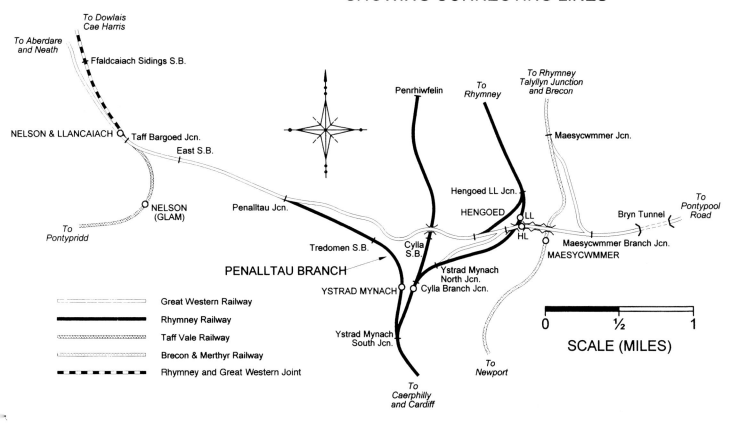

To Dowlais
Cae Harris

To Aberdare
and Neath

Ffaldcaiach Sidings S.B.

Penrhiwfelin

To
Rhymney

To Rhymney
Talyllyn Junction
and Brecon

Maesycwmmer Jcn.

NELSON & LLANCAIACH   Taff Bargoed Jcn.

East S.B.

Hengoed LL Jcn.

HENGOED

LL

To
Pontypool
Road

Bryn Tunnel

Penalltau Jcn.

NELSON
(GLAM)

HL

Maesycwmmer Branch Jcn.

To
Pontypridd

Tredomen S.B.

Cylla
S.B.

MAESYCWMMER

PENALLTAU BRANCH

Ystrad Mynach
North Jcn.

YSTRAD MYNACH   Cylla Branch Jcn.

Ystrad Mynach
South Jcn.

To
Newport

To
Caerphilly
and Cardiff

Great Western Railway

Rhymney Railway

Taff Vale Railway

Brecon & Merthyr Railway

Rhymney and Great Western Joint

0   ½   1

SCALE (MILES)

Penalltau Junction signal box controlled the branch at its upper, or north western end. The first box stood at the junction of the branch on the Vale of Neath and as there was a siding each side of the branch another box stood near the Pencarth road overbridge. These boxes were closed and replaced by a GWR box of timber construction that stood in the angle of the junction. I cannot be sure of the opening date of the new box but it was probably around 1900. What the RR paid the GWR towards the box's upkeep is also not known.

The box, with its frame facing the Penalltau branch, stood in the pleasant, marshy Caiach Valley, a quiet, tranquil tract of countryside which was a haven for wildlife. Being some distance from a public road or even a public footpath meant that the box stood in an isolated location and is probably the reason why so few photographs seem to exist of it. And since it was not connected to any mains supplies, illumination was provided by Tilley lamps. Water, for drinking and washing purposes, was delivered to the box daily by a passenger train returning empty stock from Ystrad Mynach to Dowlais (Cae Harris).

In 1923, under the scheme for grading, the box was deemed Class 4 with 110 marks. In 1937 it was still Class 4 but was given 136 marks. A new GWR pattern vertical tappet five-bar lever frame was installed in 1955. The box was provided with a switch to enable it to be closed down when not required. The GWR Service Time Tables, Pontypool Road and Neath Junction, for July-September 1935, states that the box was open from 5.00am on Mondays and closed after the last branch train on Sunday nights.

Lampman L. M. Whiteman recalls being in Penalltau Junction box some time in 1958: "I was at Penalltau to do the lamps once a week as it was part of my district. One day I was in the box with Mr. Morris, the signalman. I had gone there for the key to the lamproom. A light engine came up the branch and stopped near the box for a Vale of Neath passenger to pass. But it wasn't one of the ex-GWR '56XX' Class 0-6-2T which we usually saw. It was a gleaming ex-GWR 'Castle' Class 4-6-0 which was an unusual sight to us. I have never seen a locomotive in such glorious condition. I can't remember its name or the number, but it had been cleaned to perfection. The copper and brass shone and there was hardly a trace of smoke from the chimney. It had a perfectly built fire, haycock fashion. The driver and fireman wore ties and there was a pilot on the footplate and an inspector who wore a Homburg.

A general view of Ystrad Mynach station on the Penalltau branch, looking towards Nelson, 10th July 1958. The ex-Rhymney Railway main line is at a lower level out of picture to the right. The pine-end of the station house can be seen behind the pagoda shelter on the down platform. The single-storey dressed stone building on the up platform is of Rhymney Railway origin. (HCC/RMC)

According to the signalman, the 'Castle' was probably doing a test run before working the Royal Train to Treharris and Hirwaun a few days later."

In 1926 the Powell Duffryn Co. opened an engineering works at Tredomen, on the up side roughly halfway along the branch. The works, which manufactured mining equipment and also carried out repairs, possessed its own railway system.

Tredomen signal box, on the down side, stood opposite the two connections into the works. Brought into use in 1926, it was equipped with a twenty-lever frame. The box was a McKenzie & Holland installation which suggests that it was ordered in the final days of the RR.

It is difficult to give an accurate account of the amount of traffic into and out of Tredomen Works or how much use was made of the box. Alan James, Penalltau Junction signalman in the 1950s, recalled: "It didn't have much use during my time. When there were wagons for the works, a shunter used to go down and a signalman would open the box. It didn't take long to put a few wagons into the works as the loco could go only just beyond the gates." The works received consignments of Leighton Buzzard sand and scrap metal for the foundry. With such little use the box would therefore have been opened on an 'as required' basis. Towards the end of its useful working life

At the upper end of the Penalltau branch, where the line met the Vale of Neath at Penalltau Junction, a bridge had to be provided to carry an access road over the railway. This was the only overbridge on the line and, as can be seen, a good deal of rock had to be excavated. Out of shot and a few yards to the left, another road overbridge crossed the Vale of Neath. This photograph, looking towards Ystrad Mynach, was taken in 1972, four years after the branch had been singled. (Author)

On 10th July 1958 GWR '56XX' Class 0-6-2T No.5630 is seen dropping down the Penalltau branch to the main line at Ystrad Mynach South. The train has just left the branch platform having brought in the 4.15p.m. from Dowlais (Cae Harris). At Ystrad Mynach South, the locomotive will run round its train near the signal box which is out of shot around the curve. This view was taken from the station foot-bridge looking south towards Cardiff. The platforms on the main line at Ystrad Mynach were, and still are, staggered. Behind the down platform another member of the '56XX' Class is shunting the exchange sidings. Note the water column on the left and the carelessly-stowed drum on the platform. (HCC/RMC)

---

its windows were painted-out which suggests that its status had been reduced to that of a ground frame.

The Penalltau branch had one stopping place for passengers and this was at Ystrad Mynach. The original single-storey station building was built of dressed stone with a slate roof and stood on the up platform. It was of RR design and housed a waiting room and public conveniences. The down platform was built of timber, its shelter being in the form of a familiar GWR corrugated iron pagoda. The station was connected to the main line platforms by means of a subway which also provided access to the Brynmynach residential area.

Along the branch a number of private siding agreements were entered into. A short tramway connected Wern Ganol

Colliery to a siding at Penalltau Junction. The siding was in use for about 30 years. From 1910 Penalltau Colliery used a siding on the down side, but the date of its removal is unknown. Directly opposite the latter, a couple of sidings were provided for the small concern that was Ystrad Mynach Colliery, but these sidings were lifted just before the First World War. Below Ystrad Mynach station, on the up side, Brynmynach Siding was opened on 1st August 1914. This siding was installed to serve the Brynmynach Building Co.Ltd. The agreement was terminated on 10th June 1926.

It is not my intention here to give a comprehensive account of the traffic on this short line, but the Appendix includes an extract from the Summer 1954 working timetable.

Not all the passenger workings from Dowlais (Cae Harris) to the Rhymney Valley ran along the branch to Ystrad Mynach. Some from Dowlais ran to Hengoed (High Level) and one or two terminated at Nelson & Llancaiach.

As for the Dowlais service terminating at Ystrad Mynach, it is worth noting here that having safely dropped his passengers at the down platform, the driver of the ubiquitous ex-GWR '56XX' Class 0-6-2T was required to take his train down the branch and on to the main line to perform the run-round manoeuvre. This was carried out under the watchful eye of the Ystrad Mynach signalman directly beneath his box. I witnessed this procedure being carried out a number of times and impressively smart work it was as the locomotive and its pair of coaches were at the up platform within five minutes, in readiness for the return to Cae Harris.

Good photographs of Ystrad Mynach South signal box are comparatively rare owing to its location on an embankment remote from public access. Note the 'crank platform' in front of the box and the bracket signal with the left-hand arm off for the passing merry-go-round train to proceed on to the Penalltau Branch, the junction for which is just out of sight around the curve. In this April 1991 view, an unidentified Class 37 is hauling a rake of empties to Deep Navigation Colliery, Treharris. (R. H. Marrows)

Unlike the RR main line which saw the introduction of diesel multiple units in 1958, the Penalltau branch remained steam-hauled until the cessation of the Dowlais passenger service and the closure of the adjoining Vale of Neath through route. But as far as the branch was concerned there was one exception. It caused quite a stir and not a little interest to the schoolchildren who travelled down the branch to the grammar school at Caerphilly. In 1959 a three-car DMU traversed the branch in the down direction each weekday morning and was, to the eyes of the scholarly travellers, something of a novelty. This was the only DMU to work a publicly-advertised train over the line, having left Cardiff (Bute Road) a few hours earlier in the morning bound for Aberdare (Low Level). From the latter it travelled empty stock across the River Taff to Aberdare (High Level) on the Vale of Neath and returned to Cardiff via Quaker's Yard (High Level) and Ystrad Mynach.

On 13th June 1964 the final passenger trains ran between Dowlais and Ystrad Mynach. There being no Sunday service, the Vale of Neath was officially closed as a through route on the following Monday. As a result Penalltau Junction signal box was closed. The Penalltau branch remained in use for traffic to Taff Merthyr Colliery and Deep Navigation and for coal and foundry traffic to Cwmbargoed and Dowlais. For a few months a short length of the Vale of Neath east of Penalltau Junction was retained for use by Matissa track maintenance personnel for training purposes.

Tredomen signal box closed in 1966. The timber platform on the down side at Ystrad Mynach station was dismantled and the old RR building on the up platform demolished. The stone-faced platform was left in place and can still be seen to this day, even though it is just about hidden by mother nature.

Except for a fixed distant near the site of Penalltau Junction and a home signal at the lower end of the branch, all signalling and associated equipment was removed. The branch itself was singled in September 1968.

Following the cessation of steam at the end of 1964, the branch became the preserve of the diesel locomotive. The main player was the Type 3 English Electric, later Class 37, or 'Growler' as they have been known. Very occasionally, at times when a Taff Merthyr colliery engine had been out of action or under repair, a Radyr-based '08' Class 0-6-0 diesel mechanical shunter has been observed on the line, heading for one of the collieries to deputise for a pit locomotive under repair.

A few minutes later, following smart work at Ystrad Mynach South, No.5630 is seen entering the up platform at Ystrad Mynach on the Penalltau branch. The train then formed the 5.16pm to Nelson & Llancaiach and Dowlais (Cae Harris). The gradient through the platforms was 1 in 84 and remained so as far as Penalltau Junction. To the right of the locomotive can be seen a gateway through which a path led to a subway which connected the Penalltau branch platforms with those on the ex-Rhymney Railway main line. The houses of Brynmynach can be seen to the right. (HCC/RMC)

In August 1964 an unidentified '56XX' Class 0-6-2T, minus its smokebox numberplate, climbs towards Ystrad Mynach with a short freight. The Penalltau branch is clearly shown dropping down to the ex-Rhymney Railway main line at Ystrad Mynach South. (R. H. Marrows)

In August 1964 a '94XX' Class 0-6-0PT drifts down the branch through Ystrad Mynach with a mineral train. The platforms on the branch were sometimes erroneously referred to as 'High Level'. This was, no doubt, a local custom to distinguish the platforms in this view from the platforms on the ex-Rhymney Railway main line which were at a lower level to the right. (R. H. Marrows)

The 1 in 84 gradient is apparent in this view of the Penalltau Branch taken in August 1964, looking towards the junction with the Vale of Neath line. There were two entrances into the yard of the NCB Tredomen Works and engines were allowed to work as far as a crossing just inside the gates. Here, an unidentified GWR '56XX' Class 0-6-2T is seen propelling wagons into the works. Tredomen signal box is on the right: note the painted-out windows. (R. H. Marrows)

Between 1964 and 1977 the site of Penalltau Junction had also returned to nature and its tranquility was disturbed only by the growling of a Class 37 passing on a coal train. However, in 1977 the location was reawakened by the establishment of a National Coal Board discharge point into an area that is commonly known as the 'Nelson Bog'. This was officially called 'Nelson East Siding' where a length of track plus a loop was laid on the abandoned trackbed of the Vale of Neath. The connection to this siding faced Nelson and Class 37s were employed on spoil trains from Taff Merthyr Colliery and from the neighbouring Deep Navigation Colliery at Treharris where all tipping space had been exhausted. The siding was 37 chains in length and the procedure was for the locomotive to haul its loaded train into the siding, uncouple, run round and then slowly draw the train through the discharge point which was under the supervision of a chargeman. Two to three trains were dealt with in this fashion each day. Tipping continued until the early 1990s and ended with the eventual closure of the two collieries.

At the time of writing there is little, if any, traffic on the single line which runs from Ystrad Mynach South to the railhead and open-cast loading point at wild and windy Cwmbargoed on the desolate Dowlais Moors. But at least the Penalltau branch still exists. Today the line from Ystrad Mynach to Cwmbargoed is one long single line ten miles in length. In reality it consists of the singled Penalltau branch, one mile of the former Vale of Neath line and about seven miles of what remains of the Taff Bargoed Joint. It is worked by staff and ticket from Ystrad Mynach South. The scenery

Tredomen signal box, c1962. In this view, looking south towards Ystrad Mynach, the two connections into the Engineering Works can be seen on the right. At this time, the establishment was owned by the National Coal Board and there was little traffic into the works. Note the fixed distant signal and the loading gauge. (R. Roper)

along its entire route is attractive, but here and there appear reminders of its busier past.

3

Torpantau

A Brecon & Merthyr station in the hills

One of my everlasting regrets is that I did not travel on the Brecon & Merthyr (B&M) in South Wales. Just before the withdrawal of the passenger service between Newport and Brecon at the end of 1962, I was in a position to do so but somehow failed to get around to it. This oversight was partly made up for by my having seen much of that fascinating railway from the lineside.

The B&M was a line of contrasts and, more to the point, two distinct halves. Commencing at Newport, its southern section traversed a sizeable slice of industrial South Wales and in particular the Rhymney Valley with its numerous collieries and belching coke ovens. This major industrial valley took its name from the river which during mining's heyday ran black, its waters stained by colliery debris.

At Aberbargoed Junction, the B&M left the eastern (Monmouthshire) flank of the valley to reach Bargoed on the Glamorgan side, the River Rhymney then being the boundary between the two counties. At this station, B&M traffic used the outer face of an island platform and for the next couple of miles, having left the main line of the Rhymney Railway, ran on the metals of that company to an end-on Junction above Darran & Deri. At this place its own metals were regained. From this point northwards the B&M line was mainly single and there followed a steady climb through Fochriw and Pantywaun and on to windy Dowlais Top.

On the northern section, Dowlais Top marked the end of the B&M's twisting, uphill route through industrial south east Wales. And by the time a train had reached Pant, where a short branch ran off to Dowlais Central (formerly Lloyd Street), the traveller would have become aware that a vastly different landscape was about to be encountered. The single line from Pant, on a falling gradient to Pontsticill Junction, meant a brief respite for the engine and footplatemen as a Brecon-bound train cantered into reservoir country.

Construction of Taf Fechan reservoir (known as Pontsticill) began under a Bill put forward by Merthyr Corporation and by an Act in 1911. The contractor began work on the site in 1913. But progress was slow and during the First World War work actually ceased in 1917. Money became an issue and the delay meant that borrowing powers were required to complete the work by direct labour. The necessary Act was obtained in 1920 but in the following year Merthyr Corporation and the Rhymney Valley Authorities promoted a Bill with the same object, namely the creation of a Joint Board to take over the whole waterworks undertaking. The Taf Fechan Supply Board was constituted in 1921 formally taking over on 1st April 1922. Work recommenced and the reservoir was completed in 1927. Thus the B&M pre-dated the start of the construction of the reservoir by 50 years. The three-platform station at

An undated view of Torpantau signal box but probably during the B&M period. A poster in the window advertises market tickets. Note the extended landing at operating floor level and the hook for catching the hoop and token. (Author's Collection)

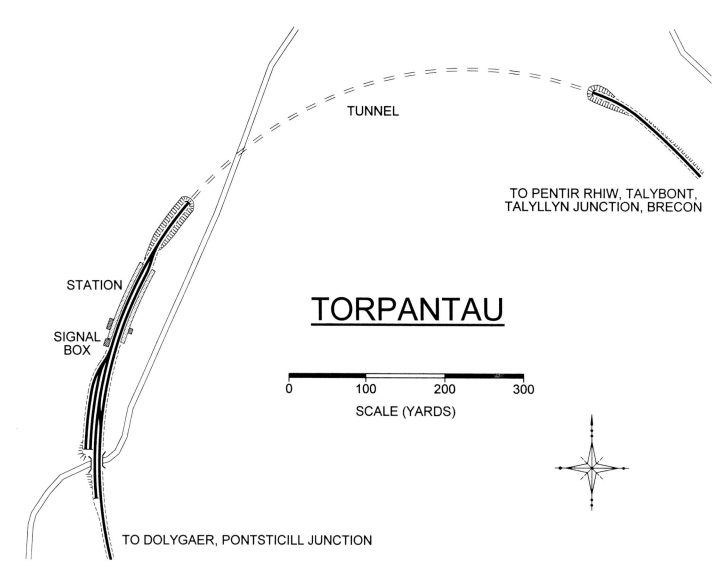

TUNNEL

TO PENTIR RHIW, TALYBONT,
TALYLLYN JUNCTION, BRECON

STATION

SIGNAL
BOX

TORPANTAU

0	100	200	300

SCALE (YARDS)

TO DOLYGAER, PONTSTICILL JUNCTION

Pontsticill Junction occupied a site on a ledge which stood about 20ft above the east shore of the reservoir and within about a hundred yards of the dam. (An early photograph exists showing a typically tranquil rural scene of a quiet agricultural landscape as a backdrop to Pontsticill Junction long before the flooding of Taf Fechan.)

Onwards along the shore of the reservoir, the line wandered through forestry plantation and into the higher ground of the Brecon Beacons, an impressive range of mountains crowned by its highest peak, Pen-y-Fan, which rises to 2,907ft. At Dolygaer, one of a number of lonely outposts of the B&M, Pentwyn reservoir was encountered. Known locally as Dolygaer Lake, this large expanse of water was constructed by the Merthyr Local Health Board in 1858. At Dolygaer the line began its escape from the Taf Fechan Valley by rising at 1 in 47 to Torpantau. An account of this station will form the bulk of this chapter and I shall return there shortly.

Beyond Torpantau Tunnel there followed, in Glyn Collwng, a spectacular seven-mile descent on a gradient of 1 in 38 through isolated Pentir Rhiw, high above Talybont Reservoir,

to the village of Talybont-on-Usk. From the latter the line rose up to Tal-y-Llyn Junction at which place B&M traffic turned west through a tunnel for the final sprint amidst rolling countryside into the quiet county town of Brecon. About two and a half hours were allowed for the journey of 47 miles during the course of which there were 22 intermediate stops. A trip on the B&M, with its contrasting scenery and steep gradients, must surely have been one of the finest railway experiences in Britain.

The foregoing gives a brief description of the route from Newport to Brecon and it is useful here to give an account of opening dates. The line was opened for passenger and freight from Brecon to Pant on 23rd April 1863. By 1st September 1868 passenger trains ran from Brecon to Newport Dock Street. (For a fuller account of opening dates concerning the entire B&M system see the bibliography.)

Roughly translated, Torpantau means 'Break in the Hollows'. This holds true at this location as the station was situated in a 'pass' or ridge between the valley of Taf Fechan to the south and Glyn Collwng to the north. The pass is

A general view of Torpantau station, looking towards Brecon, on 2nd November 1962. The red brick waiting room can be seen on the down platform. On the up platform stands the austere sand-faced single-storey station building which housed the booking office and a waiting room. The stone building at the end of the platform housed the tank for the locomotive water supply. The reservoir and valve apparatus for topping up the supply was (and still is) on the piece of level ground just below the expanse of bracken between the second and third telegraph poles. (B. J. Ashworth)

---

narrow at Torpantau and is dominated to the north west by Gorlan Tyn-y-waen and to the east by Pant-y-Creigiau (1,853ft).

I encountered Torpantau for the first time in the late 1950s. It was by chance that I came across this lonely station in the hills when, by motor car, I accompanied my father on a trip to Brecon. From that time on I had wondered why the Brecon & Merthyr company had provided a station at such an isolated spot. With the exception of a farm named Ystrad-gynwyn, half a mile away down a steep hill to the south, there was hardly any human population of which to speak. Torpantau, and for miles in every direction, was well and truly sheep country. It

was a place of rough footpaths, waterfalls, birdlife and sinus-curing medicinally fresh mountain air. Silence reigned at Torpantau, broken only by the sound of bleating sheep and occasional flurries of activity when a puffing pannier tank took a well-earned breather, having just conquered the seven-mile bank from Talybont, or when two passenger trains crossed between the platforms at five minutes past one in the afternoon. The latter event would probably have been the busiest time of day for the signalman.

During the line's construction, Mr. Henry Conybeare, the engineer to the B&M, had originally planned to excavate a 75ft-deep cutting on the ridge at Torpantau but at some point changed his mind. The Hereford Times of 13th November 1858, reported that "he now considered a tunnel to be preferable". His change of mind is understandable when one considers the amount of work and equipment that would have been required to dig such a deep cutting which would probably have needed to be about half a mile in length.

(Mr. Ben Ashworth, in a letter to the author, wrote: "I think somebody may have mentioned to Mr. Conybeare that there can be considerable quantities of snow falling at 1,300 feet in South Wales. A loco and plough would have had a problem keeping a cutting open – hence the tunnel.")

The precise opening date of the station is not known. When the line was completed a crossing loop was provided south of

On 23rd August 1962, Torpantau springs to life when two passenger trains cross at the station at five minutes past one. This photograph was taken from the 11.15am Newport to Brecon train, headed by ex-GWR '57XX' Class 0-6-0PT No.3634, which is waiting to proceed through the tunnel and on to Pentir Rhiw and Talybont. Approaching, and having just left the tunnel, is the 12.10pm Brecon-Newport headed by GWR '57XX' Class 0-6-0PT No.3747. The photographer had written on the back of this print 'weather normal' and as can be seen Torpantau on this August day was wet and gloomy. (B. J. Ashworth)

the tunnel mouth. And owing to the 1 in 38 seven-mile bank from Talybont, water facilities were installed at both ends of the loop. It is generally accepted that the station was established around 1870 and even then may have been a conditional stop only. The station consisted of two platforms with a single storey ticket office/waiting room on the up side and a brick shelter on the down. In the early days the line was worked by train staff and ticket. Signals and points were hand-worked on the ground and a crude shelter was provided for the pointsman.

In July 1892 a McKenzie & Holland signal box equipped with thirteen levers was opened on the up side at the south end of the station. The line was at this time worked by electric train tablet, the electric train token was introduced later. It was at the same time that the loop was shortened. Two sidings

immediately below the signal box, trailed into the up line. A short tramway, the gauge of which is not known, existed to the west of the station. It operated between 1918 and 1921 and was used for loading timber.

As the line ran through Torpantau on a rising gradient of 1 in 47 from Dolygaer, it was essential that the loop was clear before an up train entered the station. Added to which, with the steep bank down to Talybont very much in mind, instructions were issued concerning an up goods train leaving the north end of the tunnel. The following paragraphs are extracted from the Brecon & Merthyr Railway's Appendix to the Working Time Tables and Instructions for October 1909:

```
          TORPANTAU   STATION
In working Up Trains from Pontsticill the
Up Loop must be clear of any Train before
TRAIN  OUT  OF  SECTION  or  OBSTRUCTION
REMOVED Signal is given to Pontsticill, so
as to prevent any UP TRAIN being brought
to a STAND outside the HOME Signal.

A Bell is fixed on a Post at this Station
which must be rung by all Goods Guards
previous to their trains leaving North end
of  the  Tunnel  for  Pentir  Rhiw.  The
Signalman must acknowledge by ringing the
Bell which is placed at the North end of
the Tunnel. Any neglect of this instruc-
tion must be reported to the General
Manager.
```

On the bank behind the station and at right angles to the line stood a house which was occupied by a platelayer. Part of the premises was set aside for the storage of permanent way tools and equipment. Torpantau station was, in fact, a spartan affair with no pretensions to design, a not uncommon feature of some of the stopping places on the B&M system.

An odd feature of the station was a stone building with a slate roof cut partly into the bank at the north end of the up platform. At first sight it appeared as if it were some kind of outhouse, but the building housed the tank for the locomotive water supply. This structure was a necessary precaution to protect the supply owing to the extremely cold weather which was the predominant feature of Torpantau during winter. Water was obtained from streams running into a natural watercourse off steep-sided Gorlan Tyn-y-waen, hundreds of feet above the station. A reservoir about 40ft in diameter was provided on a piece of levelled ground above the tank. By means of a valve, housed in a brick-lined manhole alongside the reservoir, the tank on the platform was kept topped up. The tank also provided the supply to the stone water column at the south end of the loop.

At 1,313ft, Torpantau was the summit of the Brecon & Merthyr's northern section. Torpantau Tunnel, 666 yards in length, has been known by other names such as 'Beacon' tunnel and 'Summit' tunnel and was reputed to be the highest standard gauge tunnel in Britain. Within the tunnel a complete change of direction took place. For instance, traffic bound for Brecon entered the tunnel in a north easterly direction and emerged on the other side facing south east, before the helter-skelter ride down the bank to Talybont.

Installing a passing loop at Torpantau was logical when one considers the length of the section between Talybont and Pant — and with the fearsome gradient from Talybont to Torpantau, watering facilities were essential. But with so little human population in the area, why did the B&M provide a station in such an isolated place in the Brecon Beacons?

The signalman at Torpantau is about to exchange tokens with the fireman of a Brecon-Merthyr freight, headed by '57XX' Class 0-6-0PT No.9675, on 2nd November 1962. In the left background is the house which was occupied by a platelayer. To the left is a permanent way hut and the lamp room. The cast iron sign to the right of the signal box reads 'Speed must not exceed 15 miles per hour'. The expanse of clear ground in the foreground marks the site of two sidings, the last of which was taken out of use in June 1960. In the middle right of the photograph the minor road linking Pontsticill and Talybont can be seen. On the centre skyline is Craig y Fan-ddu which rises to 2,224 feet. (B. J. Ashworth)

A view of Torpantau signal box taken in 1962, the year in which the Newport—Brecon passenger service was withdrawn. Note the slate hung south pine end of the box and the net and horn for surrendering the single line token. The bleak mountainside in the background gives some idea of the isolated location of the station. The gulley running off the hill fed the reservoir for the locomotive water supply. (Nigel Hadlow)

There were two seasons only at Torpantau: a short summer and a long winter. Winters were hard and stories abound of trains becoming snowbound for days on end. The station in winter was often shrouded in mist and plagued by days of continuous sideways rain and howling winds which made life intolerable for the hardy souls employed there. There is even a story told of the signalmen at Torpantau petitioning the B&M hierarchy for the provision of a fireplace in the signal box!

Summer, on the other hand, made Torpantau a delightful beauty spot to while away a few hours of hill-walking and picnicking. The station's location alongside a minor road linking Pontsticill and Talybont-on-Usk made it ideal as an alighting point for ramblers and fishermen. Energetic residents of Merthyr, Pant and Dowlais were known to book single tickets to Torpantau in order to experience a leisurely stroll home along the narrow leafy lanes on the west shores of Pentwyn and Pontsticill Reservoirs. During the 1930s the Great Western Railway issued excursion tickets to Torpantau. In summertime, therefore, Torpantau was an attractive and popular venue for an inexpensive day out. Thus the B&M company was justified in establishing a station at that early crossing place in the hills although one can only guess at the amount of revenue the station generated.

It is not known what staffing arrangements were in place at Torpantau during the station's early days. However, in the 1950s, a porter/signalman was employed on early and late shifts.

Torpantau was in communication with Pentir Rhiw signal box to the north and Pontsticill Junction to the south, the single line being worked by electric train token. An early photograph of Torpantau signal box shows what appears to be the crudest and most fragile of token catchers. The catcher itself was fixed to an extended landing on the 'steps' end of the

In the early 1970s a stone water column, minus its bag, survived at Torpantau. This example stood on the down side at the south end of the loop. (Author)

Below:

An early 1970s view of the abandoned station at Torpantau, about ten years after closure. In this view looking south, the brick waiting room on the down platform can be seen. The minor road linking Pontsticill and Talybont can be seen in the centre of the picture. Some years after this photograph was taken, the area between the platforms was filled in and the site used for sheep gathering and dipping. (Author)

box. This arrangement was later replaced by the more familiar horn and net, with the warning of a 15mph speed restriction when surrendering and accepting the hoop and token.

The B&M passenger service between Newport and Brecon in 1910 consisted of four trains in either direction calling at Torpantau. Under the GWR in 1922 there were still four both ways, the only difference being altered calling times at the station which in most cases amounted to a matter of a few minutes. In 1938 there were four up trains and five down, one of which ran to Merthyr. In the final year there were three up trains with an extra on Saturday and three down, with two extras running as far as Bargoed, Saturdays only. During the periods mentioned, Torpantau saw a burst of activity at mid-day when two passenger trains crossed at the station. In the last timetable this interesting spectacle in the hills was booked to take place at five minutes past one. (For an example of the traffic passing through Torpantau in 1895, see Appendix.)

In the line's final years '57XX' Class 0-6-0PTs worked the passenger service between Newport and Brecon, as did the Collett '2251' Class 0-6-0s and occasionally the Ivatt Class '2'

2-6-0. Brecon shed and Newport Ebbw Junction provided the motive power.

Fireman D. W. T. Jones, better known to his colleagues as 'Bill Engine', worked as a young fireman from Merthyr shed on freight and excursion traffic through Torpantau during the 1950s. He was able to recall the procedure for working a freight train through Torpantau Tunnel and down the bank to Talybont-on-Usk:

"At Torpantau the goods train from Pontsticill would stop at the signal box. The guard fastened down some wagon brakes lightly. The train then proceeded slowly through the tunnel to a point where a cast iron notice gave the warning 'All Goods and Mineral Trains Stop Dead Here'.

"The brakes were then fastened down securely, while the driver moved the train forward until the engine was working hard against the train brakes. When the driver felt that enough brakes were secured, he sounded his whistle twice for leaving.

"All this was hidden from the signalman by the tunnel, so the guard had to press a plunger at the lineside which rang a bell in the signal box and which the signalman had to

The next station north of Torpantau. In April 1962, the Pentir Rhiw signalman exchanges tokens with the fireman of '57XX' Class 0-6-0PT No.9674. The train is the 11.15am Newport-Brecon (1.13pm at Pentir Rhiw). Note the window at the top of the signal box steps from which the signalman was able to issue tickets. Pentir Rhiw was on the seven-mile bank roughly halfway between Torpantau and Talybont-on-Usk. The station was used mainly by fishermen, walkers and members of the farming fraternity in a sparsely populated area. Apart from being a crossing place, Pentir Rhiw possessed an interesting railway feature in that, out of shot to the left, a runaway siding was provided which ran steeply into the woods behind the signal box. (Nigel Hadlow)

---

acknowledge in the same way. [*The plunger was fixed to the wall a few feet inside the Talybont end of the tunnel.*] The guard then gave the driver the 'right away'. The train proceeded down the bank on the wagon brakes, with the locomotive's and guard's van brakes in reserve... just in case! At Pentir Rhiw the points were always set for the escape line with the signal at danger.

"When the train approached Pentir Rhiw home signal, if all was well, the driver would give two crows. The signalman then reset the points and lowered the signal. At the bottom of the bank in Talybont, the brakes were released for the run up to Talyllyn Junction."

The Newport—Brecon passenger service was withdrawn on 31st December 1962. The Pontsticill Junction—Merthyr passenger service had been withdrawn over a year earlier on 13th November 1961. Torpantau signal box closed on 13th January 1963 at which date the loop and siding was taken out of use. Freight traffic continued between Merthyr and Brecon until 2nd May 1964. The exact date of dismantling of the line through Torpantau is not known, but photographs exist showing rails still in place in 1965.

I returned to Torpantau in the early 1970s. The track had long since been lifted, but the platforms were untouched. The stone water column still stood at the south end of the station. On the down platform the brick waiting room survived, almost ten years after use by the dwindling band of passengers who patronised the station. All the other railway buildings had been demolished. At the north end, the cutting leading to the tunnel, had become flooded to a depth of six inches. As the years passed, the station site was used for penning sheep before dipping, the space between the platforms being filled in.

Finally, as a footnote to this chapter and at the time of writing, it is worth noting that the Brecon Mountain Railway – which operates from Pant to Dolygaer – has laid its narrow gauge rails to Torpantau. Stop-blocks and a run-round loop have been installed a few yards south of the station. It is therefore only a matter of time before lonely Torpantau once again echoes to the sound of steam after four decades of slumber.

Pontsticill Junction was the next staff station south of Torpantau with the isolated and diminutive station at Dolygaer in between. In this view looking north, ex-GWR '57XX' 0-6-0PT No.3634 stands at the down platform with the 6.15p.m. Brecon to Newport train on 22nd August 1957. Pontsticill was the junction for Merthyr, the town being reached by way of Morlais Junction and Cefn Coed. The reservoir mentioned in the text is out of shot to the left. The village of Pontsticill stood on a hillside to the west of the reservoir and was reached by station users by means of a road across the dam. In the late 1970s Pontsticill Junction witnessed the return of steam with the establishment of the narrow gauge Brecon Mountain Railway, which in its early days ran from Pant to Pontsticill. Later, trains ran to Dolygaer, with the prospect of eventually running as far as Torpantau. The signal box has been refurbished and is in use for bed and breakfast accommodation. (Ian L. Wright)

4

Working Lives

The work of railwaymen

Apart from a general interest in the railways in the valleys of south east Wales, I have invariably had a liking for an understanding of the work railwaymen did to keep traffic running. I have discovered that retired railwaymen generally enjoy talking about their working lives. There are some who are remarkably enthusiastic and candid in their recollections of the jobs they did. On the other hand, I have come across individuals who, when approached, show little or no interest at all. To them, and I am happy to say that they are in a minority, railway work was just a job, something that paid the bills and passed the time of day.

I have met and spoken to many railwaymen, both of the retired variety and those still involved in railway work. In every case they have warmed to the subject when asked for their reminiscences. That which follows is a selection of pen pictures of those railwaymen from whom, in the course of conversations, I have learned much about the operation of a railway. The reader will discover that some men were railwaymen for an entire working lifetime whilst others left railway service due to circumstances prevailing at a particular time. One attempt at a railway career was remarkably brief, lasting less than twelve months.

E. W. Jenkins, known as Ernie to his colleagues, presented himself for possible employment on the Great Western Railway at Pontypool Road in 1910. He was interviewed by an inspector but, to Ernie's bitter disappointment, he was told to re-apply when he had grown taller.

For one year Ernie worked in a solicitor's office during which time he grew an extra inch or so. At the age of fifteen he again applied to the GWR, passed his medical examination and was accepted for railway employment. Ernie told me that being given his GWR uniform was one of the proudest moments of his life.

His first job was as a messenger boy at Pontypool Road in 1911. This lasted for about a year. His next occupation was that of a lamp lad at Nelson & Llancaiach where the station master was Mr. Walter Gilkes. Ernie respected the officious-looking Mr. Gilkes, who later became an inspector at Merthyr, and maintained that he could sometimes be stern but was always accommodating and fair-minded when dealing with his staff.

Messenger boy E. W. Jenkins, aged 15, was taken to a studio to be photographed in his GWR uniform in 1912. (Author's Collection)

GWR staff at Nelson & Llancaiach 1913, one year after the station was opened. Station master Mr. Walter Gilkes is in the middle of the front row. Lamp lad E. W. Jenkins is extreme left, back row. The policeman is Sergeant Kelland. The station changed very little over the next half century, the only noticeable change being electric lighting replacing gas at a date unknown. (Author's Collection)

Ernie experienced an example of Gilkes' compassionate nature when he allowed him to change shifts with his opposite number, a boy by the name of Beck, who for tragic family reasons was experiencing worrying times. Beck had been told that his brother was amongst those believed killed in the Universal Colliery explosion at Senghenydd in 1913 and wanted to be at the pit head to hear definite news of him.

After lamping for a few years, Ernie became a signalman and for a time lived at a railway house in Crumlin. With the experience he gained in the signal box he became a relief signalman and worked in many of the boxes between Pontypool Road and Nelson on the Vale of Neath line and on the branch to Dowlais (Cae Harris). One of the boxes he worked at as a young signalman was Gilfach Main, between Trelewis and Bedlinog on the Taff Bargoed Joint. This box was an early casualty and was closed following the reduction in traffic when steel-making at Dowlais Works ceased. However, Ernie had found his niche in the signal box and remained in that capacity until state retirement.

Signalman Ernie Jenkins pictured at Goedygric, his final signal box. After 50 years' service as a railwayman, he enjoyed almost three decades of retirement. (Author's Collection)

He once related that during his time as a relief signalman he was sent to a small box, Tyfedw, between Llanvihangel and Pandy on the Hereford line. The box was used only when the line was busy and spent a great deal of its time switched out. It had originally been opened to break the section. When he arrived there he discovered to his dismay that the box was in filthy condition. The lever frame and block instruments were coated in dust and cobwebs and a flock of birds had left its distinctive black and white autographs. On his first day at Tyfedw, he was accompanied by an inspector who arranged for him to be paid a little extra for cleaning the box. Ernie was at Tyfedw for a few months during which time he lodged locally.

His last box where he was resident signalman was at Goedygric, Pontypool, from which place he retired, aged 65, in 1961. He lived at Griffithstown and was an accomplished gardener. I became friendly with him late in his life when he came to live with his daughter in a house opposite mine. Ernie enjoyed 30 years of retirement. He died in 1991 at the grand old age of 94, after which his daughter presented me with his 1933 GWR rule book and his National Union of Railwaymen's 30 years' service badge and other service medals.

Another man to whom I have spoken is Rhondda-born Mr. Cyril Thomas. He is the eldest of six children and was a pupil at Pentre grammar school. He began work in a colliery where he had hoped to train as a mining engineer. After about a year Mr. Thomas' family doctor advised him to leave colliery work as he suffered with a weak chest which the dusty conditions underground would certainly aggravate.

In the hungry 1920s unemployment was widespread in the valleys of South Wales and Rhondda was no exception. Even in those days collieries were closing and Mr. Thomas maintained, with a wry smile, that the only businesses that could rely on regular work were furniture removers!

Undaunted, Mr. Thomas, armed with character references provided by a minister of religion and a magistrate, applied for work with the GWR. He was accepted and, as the following paragraphs will show, he embarked on a long and varied career in railway service.

On 2nd May 1928, having successfully passed his medical examination, he began work as a lad porter at Treorchy, on the Pontypridd—Treherbert line for which he was paid 17s (85p) for a six-day week. The railways were busy in Rhondda at this time and Mr. Thomas took an active interest in GWR affairs. He stated that £3 out of every £4 earned by the GWR came from the valleys of South Wales.

At first he was not made welcome by other colleagues when he became a lad porter as he had worked in the colliery. Many of the men he worked with were seasoned former Taff Vale employees. He soon discovered that a strictness existed whereby if he were told by a superior to do a job, it had to be done without question.

Mr. Thomas was able to recall that in the Rhondda Valleys, signal boxes at colliery junctions were paid for by the pit owners and in some cases the signalmen acted as checkers and were paid for taking numbers as the wagons left the pits. The colliery companies even paid for the pencils! An example of this practice was witnessed by Mr. Thomas at Maendy signal box, Ystrad, which was provided with a special window at the rear from which the signalman was able to record wagon numbers as a train drew forward from a colliery siding. Not only did the signalman receive his GWR wages but also a fee from the colliery for the added duty of recording numbers.

After a couple of years at Treorchy, Mr. Thomas moved down the line to Ystrad (Rhondda) where he worked as a porter during the Depression. There followed another move to Nantyfyllon on the Bridgend to Abergwynfi line where he was employed as a Grade 1 porter. His duties in this capacity were numerous and included booking and collecting tickets, handling parcels and attending to lamps. The station offices were illuminated by Tilley lamps.

At Aberdare during the 1930s he worked as a porter/guard which meant he spent four hours on platform duties and four hours as a guard. Yet another move followed when he went to Porth as a parcel porter. His primary duty in this capacity was to arrange parcels in their correct order, together with the relevant delivery instructions, ready for collection by the GWR carman.

Before the outbreak of the Second World War, Mr. Thomas experienced three other occupations in his long career. For a time he returned as a porter to Ystrad (Rhondda) where his wages were £2 10s (£2.50) per week. It was around this time the GWR, in a quest for greater efficiency, had plans to despatch national newspapers from Cardiff General by using road transport so, with the prospect of another change in mind, Mr. Thomas trained as a lorry driver. He was able to recall that the vehicle on which he learned to drive was a 30cwt Morris Commercial which was capable of seven miles to the gallon and needed to be filled up twice a week at Treherbert. Alas, nothing came of the GWR's intention to make newspaper deliveries by road and the plan was shelved. Shortly before hostilities broke out in 1939, Mr. Thomas returned to parcel portering.

As an experienced railwayman, Mr. Thomas was exempt from military service — or so he thought. However, owing to an oversight by a station clerk who failed to submit Mr. Thomas' exemption form, he was called up for war service and spent five years in the Royal Marines.

After the war he resumed railway work as a passenger guard at Treherbert. Mr. Thomas was quite emphatic when he told me that, like an engine driver, he too had to 'know the road'

On 3rd August 1957 ex-GWR 0-6-2T No.398 (TVR 'A' Class No.409) stands at the stopblocks at Abercynon shed. The engine was withdrawn later in the year. Also in view are '57XX' Class 0-6-0PT No.7744 and an unidentified ex-GWR '56XX' Class 0-6-2T. Note the coaling stage on the extreme left. (S. Rickard Collection/Copyright B. J. Miller)

Left:

In this view taken on 3rd August 1957, ex-GWR 0-6-2T No.383 (TVR 'A' Class No.162) is seen at Abercynon. This was another of the three-number engines withdrawn in 1957. Note the station footbridge in the background which connected the island platform with a road which ran between the down main and the shed yard. The footbridge was demolished in 1966 when it was struck violently by wagons which, following a snapped coupling, had broken away from a train ascending the bank to Quaker's Yard. (S. Rickard Collection/Copyright B. J. Miller)

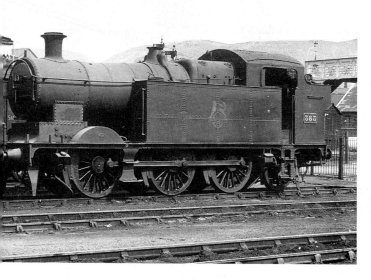

and that the driver was in charge of the locomotive but the guard had responsibility for the train. His guard duties took him to places such as Barry Island, Aberdare, Swansea, Aberavon and Merthyr. It was customary for a guard to spend a rest day on main line duties to gain experience, but Mr. Thomas was never called upon to do so.

He was able to relate to me during his time as a guard an incident which occurred that served as a reminder that some drivers left him in no doubt who was in charge of the footplate. At Barry Town station mails had been picked up but, unknown to Mr. Thomas, a group of cadets began skylarking and opened half a dozen doors on the off side of the train. The train was stopped for examination near Barry Dock and for the doors to be properly shut. However, when Mr. Thomas requested the fireman to help him secure the doors, the driver intervened and stated in no uncertain terms that "This man does not leave this engine unless I say so!"

During the 1950s Mr. Thomas applied for and obtained a foreman's job at Treherbert. Later, he took instruction in accounting and returned to Ystrad as a Class 4 clerk and shortly afterwards, because of his experience, he became a Class 3 inspector at Pontypridd. His duties there included occasional visits to Pontypridd Goods which was one of the largest goods depots in South Wales. It had a fleet of twenty lorries and deliveries were made to the Rhondda, Merthyr and Aberdare valleys.

Regrettably, Mr. Thomas stated that decline was setting in during the late 1950s. He made the interesting comment that the railways were common carriers, which meant they carried anything that was offered. Station to door deliveries were, however, becoming expensive. Drivers were paid by the number of deliveries they made or attempted to make which,

An undated view of the down side at Abercynon showing the extensive canopy over the island platform. The view is taken from the footbridge. Cardiff traffic used the down side whilst Merthyr and Aberdare used the up. The down goods line is to the left. (Author's Collection)

in effect, meant that if there was no one available at an address to receive a parcel, the driver had to go away and return at another time. This state of affairs, he said, came about because at this time women who had hitherto been at home all day had obtained factory work and as a result were not at home during the day to receive parcels.

In the mid-1960s he moved to Marland House, Cardiff, where he was employed in the despatch department. He retired in 1975 at the age of 64. At the end of his final day's work he was driven by taxi, paid for by the Western Region, to his home in Gelli, Rhondda. His colleagues made a collection to mark his retirement and with the proceeds he bought himself a typewriter. Mr. Thomas' final comment on his career was that the railway he had left was much different from the one he had joined 48 years earlier.

The work of a lengthman is sometimes overlooked except by those interested in the vital work of permanent way safety and maintenance. Mr. Thomas (Tommy) Williams joined the Hengoed permanent way gang in 1936 after enduring a string of jobs that failed as a result of the economic conditions of the time. He was medically examined by Dr. Banks of Aberdare who declared him to be fit for railway work.

The Vale of Neath line, he told me, was the GWR's second main line in South Wales and was kept in the best possible condition. As a member of the Hengoed gang, the length of line for which he and his colleagues had responsibility was

The date is 12th January 1960 and ex-GWR '56XX' Class 0-6-2T No.5601 on duty 'J6' is leaving a siding near Carn Parc box. The photograph was taken from the Carn Parc overbridge, looking south towards Stormstown Junction. Signalman Kingston, who worked in the box during this time, recalled that the box contained the biggest Romesse stove he had ever seen.
(S. Rickard Collection/Copyright B. J. Miller)

from Hengoed yard, through the station and over the viaduct to Maesycwmmer Junction, and the branch from the latter place down to the junction with the Brecon & Merthyr at Fleur-de-Lys.

He maintained that in working for the GWR he had obtained a job for life. His father was a railwayman employed by the GWR on the Aberdare relaying gang and it was a distinct advantage to be recommended for employment by a family member who was already working on the railway. Mr. Williams' career would last for a further 40 years until state retirement. It was generally accepted or acknowledged that if an employee attended regularly, was punctual and did a fair day's work to the best of his ability, the GWR was a good

company to work for, but if one stepped out of line there would be trouble and questions would be asked.

He was required to attend classes at Devon Place, Newport,

Ex-GWR '5600' Class 0-6-2T No.5601 taking water at Carn Parc, 12th January 1960. The gated siding to the right of the vans originally led to Parc Newydd Colliery, a small concern which had closed many years earlier. In this area, signalmen and shunters employed at Carn Parc and Stormstown had names for the various sidings. Those in the background, on the down side, were referred to as the 'cottages sidings' after the houses in the distance.
(S. Rickard Collection/Copyright B. J. Miller)

Carrying target J12, ex-GWR '56XX' Class 0-6-2T No. 5699, on a coal train from Penrhiwceiber, drifts through the station at Abercynon on the down relief line. Note the platform line at the end of which is the turnout for the Merthyr line. The line continuing from the points and around the curve was worked as a single line for Aberdare passenger traffic as far as Pontcynon Junction.
(B. J. Miller Collection)

where he received instruction in the work he was expected to carry out. The repair of fencing was a job undertaken by him and his colleagues in the course of their many and varied duties. It was from Mr. Williams that I learned that the fencing that runs along a railway is not necessarily the boundary between the railway company's land and that of an adjoining property owner. In some cases, especially in the countryside, the boundary could be ten, twenty or thirty feet beyond the fence. The reason for this is that if a lengthman had to carry out repairs on the outside of a fence he was not deemed to be trespassing on someone else's land.

Gangers' huts were familiar features along the lineside. They were constructed using various materials; those built with sleepers were provided with brick chimney breasts and they were useful refuges for gangers during inclement weather or when meal breaks were taken. Tools were stored overnight when gangs were working on a particular stretch of line for more than a day. The huts were also useful storerooms for the equipment and spares such as fishplates, nuts, bolts, keys and coils of fencing wire that the lengthmen required to carry out their duties.

Hedges and embankments were trimmed early in the year before birds started nesting. Cleaning culverts was another task undertaken by a lengthman as it was essential that the trackbed was properly drained. Changing rails was hard work and it could take up to twenty men to manhandle a rail into position, this sometimes being done with assistance from a neighbouring gang.

There were usually eight members of the Hengoed or Nelson gangs. The head ganger performed a daily visual inspection of the track but during high summer he walked his stretch of

track twice daily. After nationalisation the man who inspected the track was known as a patrolman and he was paid a sub-ganger's rate. It was the responsibility of the permanent way inspector to check the track for gauge.

Near Penalltau Junction, there was a stretch of track which required special attention as it was laid on wet, peaty ground in which there were ribs of rock in various places. Much time was spent at this location, lifting and packing the track to keep it straight and level.

The hunting fraternity could sometimes cause extra work for the gang and relations between hunters and gangers were invariably strained. Mr. Williams once witnessed a hunt master with the pack actually on the line at Pencarth. A fox had got into a culvert and was working its way down towards the Penalltau branch. The master even asked the head ganger if he could have the train stopped but the boards were off and by this time the pack, eager for the kill, was on the line. Nothing could be done to stop the Pontypool Road—Aberdare train. It emerged around a curve, passed beneath a road overbridge and ploughed into the pack in what turned out to be a bloodbath. Eight of the dogs were killed.

On another occasion, the hunt master, on discovering that the gates were locked on either side of the line, deliberately cut fence wires so that the pack could cross to the other side. The fence wires were tensioned and when cut they sprang in all directions, in some cases becoming entangled with lineside equipment. It was following this incident that the farmer banned the hunt from his land.

The winter of 1947 tested to the limit railwaymen of all occupations and, according to Mr. Williams, permanent way staff endured the vilest of weather. Long hours were spent

On 27th August 1948 GWR 0-6-2T No. 282 (ex-TVR No. 9) is seen standing in a siding north of Abercynon with the Aberdare branch train. Abercynon station is out of shot to the right and once a Cardiff—Merthyr train had left the up platform, the Aberdare train would set back into the platform to pick up passengers for the Aberdare branch. The incline to Quaker's Yard can be seen behind the bracket signal on the left. The tall chimney on the right indicates the location of Abercynon Colliery. (Ian L. Wright)

keeping pointwork and rodding clear of snow and there were occasions, during falling snow, when he acted as a fog signalman. The brutal, Arctic weather took its toll on his health. He became ill for the first and only time in his working life, having to take time off work and spending a month in hospital. He had suffered kidney failure, which the specialist attributed to the effects of the weather in that dreadful winter. Before he returned to work, the GWR insisted that he took a fortnight's holiday.

In 1964, following the closure of the Vale of Neath, the Hengoed gang was disbanded. There were redundancies, but owing to Mr. Williams' length of service, he was retained and became a member of the newly-formed Dowlais gang. This gang earned for itself the nickname 'Mountain Boys', no doubt because they were employed on the steeply-graded line to Cwmbargoed and Dowlais, and anyone who knows the isolated location of Cwmbargoed will understand what was meant by the nickname.

In this undated view taken at Abercynon, BR '16XX' Class 0-6-0PT No. 1612, is seen on the coal road along with an unidentified member of the '56XX' Class and an 0-6-0PT. No. 1612 was built in 1949 and withdrawn in 1965. (L. F. Waters)

But conditions were altering for Mr. Williams and his colleagues. Steam had gone and the only traffic they saw was coal trains hauled by the new diesel locomotives. The railway he had joined had changed. However, one change of which he did approve made the Mountain Boys' lives much easier. Instead of walking along the line to the location of the day's work, they were driven, courtesy of the internal combustion engine. A brand-new BMC diesel, painted yellow, was provided. It picked the gang up in the morning and took them to their place of work. Mr. Williams recalled that it was a big vehicle that not only carried their tools but was also equipped with cooking facilities. When the line from Nelson to Dowlais was singled in the mid-1960s, it was possible to drive the vehicle over the ballast from Dowlais to Bedlinog. Travelling in the vehicle meant they did little walking and made less use of the lineside huts.

But one of the lineside huts the gang *did* use on a regular basis was located near a place called 'Club Row' after a street of terraced houses near Taff Merthyr Colliery. It was whilst working here that the Mountain Boys discovered a thin seam of coal which came to the surface near the line. Coal from this seam kept a fire going in the hut for some time.

Towards the end of his working career, a system which Mr. Williams loosely described as 'payments by results' was introduced. This was a method of planning work to be done which entailed a certain amount of paperwork and calculation so that a time could be estimated for a particular piece of work. For example, a 100 yards culvert which had to be cleaned was allowed, say, four hours, or a day was allowed for the cutting of embankment undergrowth. By giving an estimate of tasks to be undertaken it was assumed that work could be planned more efficiently.

In modest fashion, Mr. Williams stated that he had always had an aptitude for mathematics and, following a few days' course at Devon Place, Newport, discovered that the forms associated with the new method of timing work to be done presented him with no particular problems. He found the forms easy to understand and complete. Trial estimates that he undertook were eventually considered to be reasonably accurate. Such was his proficiency that he was asked by superiors to follow up the course with practical experience.

Not all permanent way men, though, were enthusiastic about the new method. On one occasion, Mr. Williams was sent to Ystrad Mynach to estimate a piece of work that needed doing. A complaint had been received from a shunter who was continually getting his legs wet when shunting near an embankment alongside a siding. The work involved cutting the base of the embankment back a few feet using a pick and shovel. When a ganger was requested by Mr. Williams to cut back about twenty yards of embankment, he steadfastly refused, stating that he was not prepared to work supervised by a man armed with a stopwatch! However, a more enlightened ganger, burly Richard 'Dick' Lewis, readily agreed to do the work and completed the task easily within the time allowed by Mr. Williams.

Such was his success at estimating work to be done that Mr. Williams was asked by his superior if he would like to become involved on a full-time basis. Old habits die hard, though, and

Mr. Williams declined, stating that he preferred the outdoor life and had no desire to become a pen-pusher.

Tommy Williams retired with a railway pension in 1976 at the age of 65. To mark his 40 years' service the district office sent him a wristwatch but there was no formal presentation.

Abercynon shed, between Merthyr and Cardiff on the ex-Taff Vale main line, was built under the Loans & Guarantees Act 1929. The new two-road shed replaced an earlier small Taff Vale depot which stood on the down side of the line. Mr. Ron Yeo obtained employment at the shed in 1943 when he was fifteen years of age. Like other railwaymen, the fact that he had a relation working on the Great Western at Cardiff helped him secure the job. He had to wait a few weeks before his application was accepted but was told that he could start work as an engine cleaner.

He was given two denim uniforms. One was worn while the other was being washed and since his job entailed clambering around engines the uniform he wore did not stay clean for long. He worked three shifts but on nights his first duty was to act as a knocker-up. Armed with a list of names and addresses he trudged the terraced streets of Abercynon at all hours of the night. Drivers, firemen and guards had to be knocked-up depending on what time they were booked to sign on. He was required to knock on the front door, no matter how long it took, until he got an answer either from the man or from the lady of the house.

The engines at Abercynon were of the '56XX' Class 0-6-2Ts, 0-6-0PTs and some of the old ex-Taff Vale 0-6-2 three-number tanks. He was issued daily with a wad of cotton waste and oil for cleaning purposes that had to last for the shift. There were occasions when the drudgery of engine cleaning was relieved when he was sent to Caerphilly Works by train carrying worn big end brasses so that they could be exchanged for a new set.

When he became a fireman he had to learn the road and know exactly when the driver required maximum steam. Most of his firing turns were in the yard and on the banker from Stormstown Junction up the big bank to Quaker's Yard.

Although not keen to leave Abercynon, after about eighteen months Mr. Yeo was transferred by the GWR to Old Oak Common. At Old Oak he found himself in a completely different world after working with tank engines in the valleys, but at least the move to London gave him experience firing the bigger engines. He fired 'Halls', 'Castles' and the locomotives that impressed him most, the 'Kings'. He fired occasionally on the main line as far as Reading and Didcot and into Paddington.

Following National Service he resumed railway work at Worcester by which time the railways had been nationalised. He soon obtained a compassionate transfer back to Abercynon but with prospects of marriage, he left British Railways to earn better wages at the coal face of Deep Navigation Colliery, Treharris, a pit noted for its production of top quality steam

A c1962 view of the down platform at Hengoed (High Level), looking across the viaduct towards Pontllanfraith and Pontypool Road. The permanent way through the station and over the viaduct to Maesycwmmer Junction was the responsibility of the Hengoed gang. (R. Roper)

BELOW: *In April 1993 a pair of Class 37s, with No.37 802 leading, approach the 'Club Row' road overbridge with a train of merry-go-round empties for Cwmbargoed. As mentioned in the text, it was in the late 1960s at this location that the 'Mountain Boys' discovered a thin seam of coal which was used to keep the fire going in one of their lineside huts. The tail of the train indicates the site of Taff Merthyr Colliery Halt. The colliery occupies the lower ground of the Taff Bargoed Valley.*
(R. H. Marrows)

In his reminiscences, lampman L. M. Whiteman mentioned that he was required to maintain the signal lamps at Bedlinog even though, for a short time, they were permanently in the off position. Here, in 1964, ex-GWR '56XX' Class 0-6-2T No.5618 climbs through the station with a rake of 20-ton vacuum-fitted wagons for Cwmbargoed. (R. H. Marrows)

coal. Ironically, the coal Mr. Yeo dug in the Nine Feet seam at Deep Navigation was the locomotive coal that was supplied to Abercynon shed.

I mentioned earlier that when a man applied for railway employment it was a distinct advantage if a member of his family was already employed in railway work. However, in Mr. William Lucas' case, since he had no relation working as a railwayman, he was required by the GWR to provide two character references preferably from an inspector of police, a minister of the church or a Justice of the Peace.

He began work in May 1944 as a lad porter at Aberfan on the Quaker's Yard & Merthyr Joint line which ran up the western flank of the Taff Valley. The line closed suddenly in

1951 owing to the instability of Joint Line viaduct at Quaker's Yard. This former GWR/Rhymney Railway line was never more than half a mile from the ex-Taff Vale main line that ran to Merthyr on the opposite side of the valley.

Amongst his many duties as a lad porter he spent much of his time handling parcels. He recalled his wages were £1 10s 9d (£1.54) per week and each fortnight he paid 1s 3d (7p) into the GWR pension fund.

Mr. Lucas not only worked at Aberfan, but split his duties between Merthyr Vale and Troedyrhiw stations on the ex-Taff Vale line. He recalled that the glasses on the gas lamps on the platforms at Aberfan during the war were painted blue. One of his occasional duties was to deliver soap, polish and other items to Merthyr Vale Junction signal box. During the Second World War this box — which controlled the connection into Merthyr Vale colliery, via a viaduct over the River Taff—was worked by two women, Mrs. Wall and Mrs. Wills. There was good-natured competition between the two ladies to see who could keep the box the cleaner. The signal ladies were replaced by men when hostilities ceased.

Mr. Lucas was a railwayman all his working life and at retirement he could still quote without hesitation some of the

A general view of Abercynon shed, October 1963.
(R. H. Marrows)

train fares of 50 years earlier: From Aberfan it was 9d return to Merthyr. A day return to Paddington was £1 14s (£1.70) and it was 2s 9d (14p) return from Aberfan to Cardiff Bute Road via Ystrad Mynach. Mr. Lucas also spoke of what he considered to be his claim to fame. It was whilst working at Merthyr Vale as a porter that he was visited one day by a detective who was making enquiries concerning the 10 Rillington Place murders case. Mr. Lucas had to confirm to the detective that he had sold Timothy Evans, who was wrongly hanged for murder, a ticket to Paddington. He was probably the last of the local population to see Evans alive.

Mr. Lucas ended his career as a railwayman in the early 1990s. The greater part of his working life was spent as a passenger guard on the valley lines.

Mr. John Lintern was taken on at Caerphilly Works in 1951 after he had left school. Again, as with others, personal recommendation played a major part in his being accepted for employment. At first he was paid £1 1s (£1.05) a week and worked as a foreman's boy, which was the polite title for the post of office boy. He was given a metal pay cheque and had to stand in line to receive his wages.

Later he worked as a steam hammer operator in the Smith Shop. Then he began his apprenticeship as a welder which meant he worked in both the Smith Shop and the Erecting Shop, most of his time being spent on repairs to locomotives. As an apprentice, his attendance at night school was compulsory.

He recalled that there was a single line from the east end of Caerphilly station which was sometimes referred to as the test line. It was the only entrance into the works. Apart from the workmen's trains from Newport and Cardiff, and locomotives entering the yard, the line was used to test engines after they had come out of the works following repair.

Caerphilly Works, known locally as 'The Sheds', closed on 28th June 1963 and Mr. Lintern was able to recall some sad sights in the Smith and Spring shops such as heaps of discarded tools on the shop floor. With the closure of Caerphilly Works, Mr. Lintern left railway work.

One summer evening in 1955, Mr. Leighton M. Whiteman was advised by his railwayman father that there was a vacancy for a lampman on the Vale of Neath. At seventeen years of age, Mr. Whiteman had already worked as a cinema rewind boy and as an assistant in a gentlemen's outfitters but dissatisfied with the work he had done, he decided to apply for the job. I mentioned earlier that Thomas Williams, the lengthman, had been examined by Dr. Banks of Aberdare. Two decades later, Dr. Banks was still acting for the railway and also passed Mr. Whiteman as fit for railway work.

Inspector Tom Jones interviewed Mr. Whiteman and gave him a copy of the British Railways rule book with which he was expected to become familiar and on which he was tested from time to time. He undertook instructions into the secrets of the lampman from a senior man, Ivor Thomas, and he discovered that apart from lamping, safety was paramount. After a fortnight of instruction, Mr. Whiteman was considered competent enough to undertake the task of lampman alone. After three months at the job he was summoned to Pontypool Road where an inspector confirmed that his position was permanent.

In April 1963 DMUs occupy each side of the island platform at Abercynon. In this view looking north, a Cardiff-bound train stands on the down side (right) whilst on the up is a train for Merthyr. The signal box appears in its original all-timber form with a cast iron nameplate on each side. The plate on the up side was rescued many years later and affixed to the back interior wall of the box. (R. H. Marrows)

His district was from Mountain Ash (Cardiff Road) to Penalltau Junction, including the down distant on the Penalltau branch. He worked a six day week — five and a half to be precise — finishing at 12 noon on Saturdays.

I learned from Mr. Whiteman that all the lamp rooms were constructed, for reasons which are obvious, of corrugated iron on an angle iron frame. The floor was of flagstone or brick. A steel bench was provided as a working area when lamps were cleaned and filled. The only item of wood in the lamp room was the horse upon which the paraffin barrel rested. Paraffin was supplied on a six-monthly contract and was either Shell Pink or Esso Blue depending on the supplier.

Keys to the lamp rooms in his district were kept at the nearest station or signal box. It was the responsibility of the

station master of the station to which Mr. Whiteman was attached to provide a supply of England's Glory safety matches. Time sheets were required to be completed weekly. On one occasion, Mr. Whiteman incurred the wrath of the station clerk at Quaker's Yard who returned his time sheet and ordered him to rewrite it using either blue or black ink as he had filled in his sheet using a green pen which was the railway auditor's colour.

It was strictly forbidden for a lamp to be filled and cleaned on the signal post. This had to be done in the lamp room and there was a routine procedure to observe. A lamp for filling was removed from the post and replaced by one that had already received attention. The lamp requiring maintenance was placed on the bench. The wick was trimmed, the burner cleaned and the front and rear glasses given a wipe over. The filler cap was removed and placed beneath the lamp which caused it to tilt making it easier to observe the paraffin level. The cap was replaced and the lamp lit. Then the flame was adjusted to a mark on the glass to get the flame level and was allowed to burn for twenty minutes. The only other job Mr. Whiteman did whilst on the landing of a signal post was to clean the signal arm aspects.

Walking along the permanent way could at times be hazardous. Mr. Whiteman recalled that there was one place in particular in which he felt uneasy and that was in the single bore Quaker's Yard West Tunnel. It was about 700 yards in length and straight except for a slight curve at the Penrhiwceiber end. The clearance in the tunnel was tight and there was only about one foot between the top of an engine's chimney and the roof of the tunnel. It is therefore not difficult for the reader to imagine the amount of choking smoke, steam and cinders that hit the roof especially when an eastbound freight, with assistance from a banking engine, was pounding up the 1 in 100 gradient towards Quaker's Yard.

To make matters worse, the tunnel was unventilated. Manholes were provided at regular intervals on both sides and halfway along the tunnel on the down side was a platelayers' cabin or refuge which had been hewn from solid rock.

One day early in his lamping career, Mr. Whiteman was walking through the tunnel towards Quaker's Yard (High Level) when he heard, behind him, the whistle of a locomotive as it entered the tunnel from the Penrhiwceiber end. He leaned back into one of the manholes and waited for the train to pass. Owing to the limited clearance, smoke and fumes hung about long after a train had passed and he thought that this particular train had safely cleared. Thinking that it was safe to proceed, he heaved himself from the manhole but discovered, to his horror, that he could just about hear the bark from the banking engine. He immediately returned to the safety of the manhole. Mr. Whiteman learned a valuable lesson in that the smoke from the train engine, which happened to be a 'Grange' on that occasion, deadened the sound of the following banking engine.

After that unnerving experience, he decided a week later to avoid the tunnel and walk to Quaker's Yard over the steep-sided Cefn Glas mountain, following the telegraph poles through the ferns, but this took the best part of an hour, whereas the walk through the tunnel took about twenty minutes.

Mr. Whiteman maintained that windy weather and falling snow were the biggest enemies of the lampman and that lighting a lamp on a swaying 30ft high signal post could at times be unnerving. The extraordinarily tall up inner home at Nelson always proved difficult until it was moved, for sighting purposes, to another position.

He came across occasional evidence of vandalism. He recalled that at Penalltau Junction, the Nelson down distant stood only a few yards from a road overbridge. The signal was an inviting target for hunters who frequented the surrounding marshy area. Armed with twelve-bore shotguns, they chose to use the signal for practice. At times, the lamp had been peppered with so much shot that it was difficult to remove it from its bracket.

Some signals, especially those that stood on a platform, had to be made safe from the attentions of the more adventurous members of the travelling public. The up main platform starter at Nelson had its ladder shortened, the final eight feet to platform level being removed, thus preventing anyone with an idea of skylarking from climbing the signal. A wooden ladder was kept padlocked to the signal post and this was used to reach the fixed ladder when lamps required attention.

In 1964, following the closure of the Vale of Neath, unlike some of his colleagues, Mr. Whiteman was not made redundant. However, his district was greatly reduced and he worked on the Dowlais line for about a year. He was even instructed to maintain lamps at Bedlinog even though, for a time, they were permanently off and drivers took little or no notice of them.

With a bleak future in prospect, he took a British Railways driving course at Taplow and for a short time acted as a porter at Merthyr. Disillusioned, he ceased to be railwayman in 1965.

My final question to Mr. Whiteman was "Why were you a lampman for ten years?" I had always understood that it was a job from which a man progressed to, say, the signal box. His reply was typically straight to the point when he stated that he enjoyed working days regularly and had no desire whatsoever to work shifts. He added that being a lampman meant that he was his own boss, worked unsupervised and, except for an occasional eyesight test conducted at the side of the line by an inspector, he rarely saw anyone in authority. In ten years of lamping, Mr. Whiteman encountered the Swindon lamp inspector once only.

Some men who took up railway work in the early 1950s were unaware at the time that they would witness great changes in the years that would follow. Mr. Norman Kingston began work as a lamp lad at Pontypridd in 1954 when the railway he joined had changed very little during the preceding half century. Most of the lines in the valleys were still in use although the auto-worked passenger service from Pontypridd to Ynysybwl had been withdrawn three years earlier. The diesel locomotive and the diesel multiple unit had yet to make their appearances in the valleys of South Wales and pre-grouping engines were still at work on passenger and coal traffic.

Mr. Kingston worked as a lamp lad for just under two years. His early years as a railwayman, he told me, were enjoyable and an abiding memory during the course of his daily duties was being at PC&N Junction on a warm, sunny, summer morning and experiencing the aroma of creosote rising from the sleepers. It was, he added, an experience he has never forgotten. For about six months he was a temporary porter at Pontypridd. In 1958, after National Service, he became a resident signalman at Ynyshir on the Maerdy branch.

But it was while he was at Carn Parc signal box in 1962 that

On a dreary day in July 1964, an enthusiasts' excursion, hauled by a member of the '56XX' class, enters the up platform at Abercynon. On the down relief line an engine of the same class trundles south with a coal train.
(R. H. Marrows)

he realised the railway he had joined was changing rapidly. Diesel multiple units had begun working passengers to Merthyr in 1958 but freight was still in the hands of the steam engine. He was on early shift when he received a telephone call from an inspector who told him that a train of empties for Merthyr Vale Colliery was being worked that morning by one of the new diesel locomotives. The inspector requested that the banking engine be kept in a siding at Carn Parc in case the diesel needed assistance through Abercynon and up the bank to Quaker's Yard.

The brand-new diesel growled impressively past the box and disappeared around the curve towards Abercynon. Ten minutes later the signalman at Abercynon rang Mr. Kingston to inform him that the banking engine would not be required as the diesel had taken its train up the bank with ease and had reached Quaker's Yard in half the usual time. It was the appearance of that diesel locomotive working the train of empties to Merthyr Vale which finally convinced Mr. Kingston that the railway he had joined was fast changing.

Later, Mr. Kingston worked at Pont Shon Norton Junction and Llandaff Loop signal boxes. His final box was Abercynon where he worked for seventeen years. He retired in 1999.

Every man who applied for employment on the railway was required to undergo a medical examination and this was usually undertaken locally or not too far from home. But Mr. Hugh Williams, a 15-year-old school leaver in 1960, had to travel to Swindon for his medical. Following a successful visit to the railway doctor, he took up employment as an engine cleaner at Abercynon and at first earned £3 10s (£3.50) a week. As part of his training he attended lessons in a disused shunters' cabin near Barry Town station.

Back at Abercynon, the shedmaster asked him rudimentary questions about the working of a steam locomotive. He also tested him on the rules, in particular Rule 55. He wasn't allowed to go on to a locomotive until he was a passed cleaner and his first turn in that position was on the Stormstown pilot. Mr. Williams recalled firing on the banking engine that gave the required push to assist a heavy train up the bank to Quaker's Yard. It was hard work all the way but on the viaduct south of Low Level station the banking engine gently eased off then came to a stand beyond the dummy by Low Level box, ran back over the crossover on to the down line and returned to Abercynon.

He was made fireman in 1961 and was paid £7 a week. He was paired permanently with a driver and worked in the Aberdare Valley and to Merthyr. As was common when employed in railway work, he started his shifts at all hours and got used to haphazard sleeping patterns. One early turn with which he became familiar meant a 2.30am start. It was light engine down to Carn Parc where he and the driver waited for the mail train to Aberdare. The mail was uncoupled and attached to five empty coaches which were taken to Merthyr running as empty stock. Later in the morning the coaches formed the 7.20am Merthyr—Pontypridd passenger.

Mr. Williams was able to recall, for special reasons, two Abercynon engines which he fired. The first was ex-GWR '56XX' Class 0-6-2T No.5680 which was kept and specially cleaned for Aberavon excursions. The second was an engine of the same class, No.5601, which was involved in a wild run and on which Mr. Williams was firing when it got out of control on Quaker's Yard bank. Overpowered by its heavy load, the train roared through Abercynon station and finally came to a stand at Carn Parc. Following this hair-raising incident, Mr. Williams and his driver were summoned to Marland House, Cardiff, where they were interviewed by the train inspector. Apart from a reprimand no further action was taken.

Mr. Williams was one of those young railwaymen who witnessed the upheavels and changes of the 1960s. Abercynon shed was closed in November 1964. He recalled firing No.5699 when it took 0-6-0PTs No.7744 and No.9622 to Woodham's Yard, Barry, for scrapping.

I learned from him that following closure of the shed, Abercynon was retained as a signing-on point until 1968. Train crews used a room in the station building on the big island platform. In 1974 he ended his railway career after spells at Radyr and as a passenger guard at Treherbert.

There were those, I discovered, who for reasons of their own spent only a short time in railway service. One such individual was Mr. Gareth Fear who left school in 1959. At first he spent a year working at Llanwern, near Newport, when the Spencer steelworks was under construction. When his job at the steelworks came to an end, he decided to consider a career in railway work. It was a career that would last less than a year.

In 1960 he heard by word of mouth that there were some vacancies for engine cleaners at Abercynon shed. He did not write a letter of application but cycled to the shed, made enquiries and was interviewed by the shedmaster, a man whom he discovered everyone referred to as 'The Boss'. His interview successful, he was sent to Cardiff where he passed a medical examination. His next port of call was Canton where he was provided with two denim uniforms, a cap and a copy of the British Railways rule book.

Abercynon in 1960 had an allocation of ex-GWR '56XX' Class 0-6-2Ts and 0-6-0PTs and these engines were employed on freight and passenger work to Aberdare, Merthyr and Pontypridd, shunting at Stormstown yard and banking duties to Quaker's Yard. Mr. Fear's job as a cleaner was not confined to engines, which were cleaned both outside and underneath. He was responsible for filling the sand boxes and at times was required to help out when locomotives were being coaled and watered. He was issued each morning with a wad of cotton waste, which he referred to as rags, and an amount of paraffin for cleaning purposes. He recalled that his wages were given to him by the foreman each Friday in the shed canteen.

From what he told me the Western Region of British Railways was having difficulty attracting boys and men to become cleaners and then firemen. Such was the shortage that Mr. Fear was sent for a fortnight to Aberdare shed where he undertook a crash course to become a fireman. At Aberdare he was taught the art of firing a locomotive, the maintenance of the water level, the passage of steam from the boiler to the chimney and the other sundry duties expected of a fireman when on the footplate.

For a short time back at Abercynon, Mr. Fear fired on some of the turns to Ynysybwl and at Stormstown yard. His time at Abercynon did not last long, though, for a vacancy list appeared and he and five of his colleagues moved elsewhere. He obtained a transfer to Severn Tunnel Junction where he lodged in the British Railways hostel. Severn Tunnel Junction employed many men who made use of the staff canteen, an establishment which was open all hours and which provided footplate crews with packed sandwiches.

His stay at Severn Tunnel was brief, about three months during which he recalled firing through the Severn Tunnel to Pilning and in Severn Tunnel yard. Although he enjoyed his work the wages were poor and at the tender age of seventeen he left railway service to join the Army.

Class 37 No.37 889 passing Abercynon signal box with a train of empties for Tower Colliery in March 1991. Note the starter signals, with the left hand arm off indicating the imminent arrival/departure of a Merthyr—Cardiff train.
(R. H. Marrows)

5

Diesels at Ocean

A location on the Vale of Neath passes into history

To the railwaymen of south east Wales it was known as 'Ocean', to the local population it was a place of grimy, hard work and to the railway historian a location in East Glamorgan where two collieries made connections with the Vale of Neath (VoN). The purpose of this chapter is to recall the development of Ocean and Taff Merthyr Collieries Junction from its early days through to its closure and complete abandonment in the mid-1990s, a time when one of a few surviving sections of the VoN was finally lost for ever. As will be evident and as the title suggests, the pictorial content will, in the main, cover the final 30 years of locomotive activity at Ocean when the Class 37 diesels reigned supreme.

The Taff Vale Extension Railway, constructed by the Newport, Abergavenny & Hereford Railway, was opened throughout from Pontypool to Quaker's Yard in 1858. It was a spectacular double line, an engineering wonder which included lofty Crumlin Viaduct over the Ebbw Valley and the masonry masterpiece, Hengoed Viaduct, which still strides elegantly over the Rhymney Valley almost 40 years since the last train steamed eastward to Pontypool. Following a short period of ownership by the West Midland Railway, the line became part of the Great Western in 1864. At this time the line was extended through Cefn Glas tunnel into the Aberdare Valley and an end-on junction was made with the Vale of Neath at Middle Duffryn, near Mountain Ash. The line from Pontypool to Neath became the GWR's second main line in South Wales.

At Treharris the VoN, which in its tortuous route from Pontypool had already crossed three river valleys and had traversed the marshy Caiach Valley, suddenly turned through more than ninety degrees to run on a shelf hewn out of a hillside to reach Quaker's Yard. (Curves abounded at Treharris: between Trelewis and the VoN viaduct at Quaker's Yard – a distance of a little under two miles – there was hardly a length of straight track.)

The reader will observe that I have already mentioned Treharris. I have done this purely to fix the village's location for, in 1858, Treharris as a settlement did not exist. The double line at that time ran through a virtually unspoilt rural landscape of babbling brooks, steep-sided wooded hills, farm tracks and the Taff Bargoed River which at Quaker's Yard tumbled into the River Taff. Apart from embankments and one or two occupation crossings, the only notable engineering feature of the line in the area under review was Treharris Viaduct. Built on a tight curve, the dressed-stone viaduct was 78 yards in length and its three arches carried the line over the Taff Bargoed River. Before the development of colliery workings the viaduct was considered the centrepiece of an area of outstanding natural beauty and has been featured several times in early postcard views. The tranquillity of the landscape was broken only by the Neath—Aberdare—Pontypool trains that steamed by on the plain track of the VoN.

That peace was shattered in 1873, when a group of businessmen led by F. W. Harris sank mine shafts following the purchase of a mineral lease on 3,500 acres of land owned by Pantanas, Cefn Forrest and Twyn-y-Garreg farms. It was a risky venture and towards the end of sinking operations the owners actually ran out of money. However, persistence paid and in 1879 the first high-quality steam coal was wound to the surface. Less than twenty years later the workforce had grown to 2,500 men who were producing 600,000 tons of coal annually. The mine was known as Harris' Navigation Colliery and the village that grew alongside it became Treharris (Harris' Town) after F. W. Harris. For many years 'Deep Navvy', as the local population called it, was the deepest mine in Wales.

Laying the colliery connection was a relatively simple affair. The VoN had pre-dated the colliery by fifteen years and the pit buildings, sidings, shafts and engine house were no more than a stone's throw from the line. The junction faced west and a couple of sidings were provided on the up side. Additional sidings were added, again on the up side, nearer Treharris station which, to serve the growing mining village, was opened to the public in 1890. The Ocean Coal Company Ltd. bought out the Harris concern in 1893 and it renamed the pit Deep Navigation Colliery.

Records show that Harris Navigation signal box appears to have been in use in 1875. It stood on the up side. Space was at a premium at the junction and the box, of timber and stone construction, backed tightly on to a colliery retaining wall. Trains of empties arriving at the colliery on the up side were

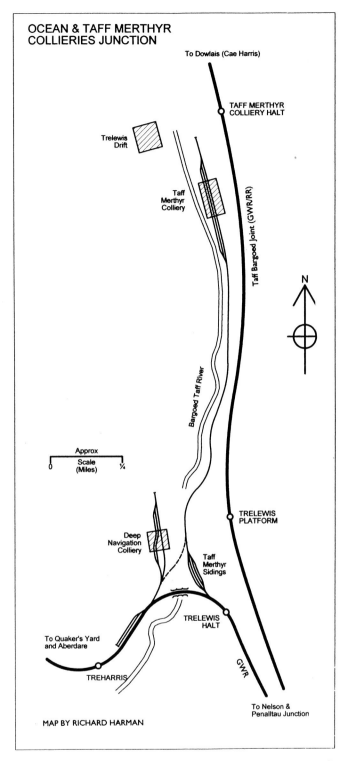

OCEAN & TAFF MERTHYR
COLLIERIES JUNCTION

To Dowlais (Cae Harris)

TAFF MERTHYR
COLLIERY HALT

Trelewis
Drift

Taff
Merthyr
Colliery

Taff Bargoed Joint (GWR/RR)

N

Bargoed Taff River

Approx
Scale
(Miles)
0   ¼

TRELEWIS
PLATFORM

Deep
Navigation
Colliery

Taff
Merthyr
Sidings

To Quaker's Yard
and Aberdare

TRELEWIS
HALT

TREHARRIS

GWR

To Nelson &
Penalltau Junction

MAP BY RICHARD HARMAN

Many years later and further north about a mile away in the Taff Bargoed Valley, a new pit was beginning to take shape. This was Taff Merthyr Colliery, a joint venture between the Powell Duffryn Company and the Ocean Coal Company. Sinking operations began in 1922 and at that time the colliery was considered the most modern in South Wales.

The Taff Bargoed Railway, a joint undertaking between the GWR and the Rhymney Railway, had been brought into use in 1876 primarily for the transport of iron ore to Dowlais Works. But since that steeply-graded double line, which ran from Llancaiach to Dowlais, ran on a ledge cut into the eastern flank of the valley, it was not possible to connect Taff Merthyr Colliery to that line. The line was at a considerably higher level than the new colliery which was established at river level.

To provide a rail connection with Taff Merthyr Colliery a single line branch a little over a mile long was constructed. It left the VoN on the eastern side of Treharris viaduct and wriggled its way behind the slate-roofed village of Trelewis. Further north it followed the Taff Bargoed River (which had been diverted to accommodate the colliery buildings and sidings) before finally coming to an abrupt end at stopblocks at the north end of the colliery yard. Materials for the construction of the colliery were carried along the branch, the junction for the line being controlled by Taff Merthyr Colliery Sidings Ground Frame.

Towards the end of the sinking and development of Taff Merthyr Colliery, the General Strike of 1926 occurred. A great deal of money had been invested in the new colliery but, despite the strike, an agreement between capital and labour was reached which allowed the development of the pit to continue unhindered. The first high-quality steam coal was lifted to the surface shortly after the end of the strike.

I mentioned earlier that the Taff Bargoed line passed Taff Merthyr Colliery at a higher level and that a freight connection was impossible. But at least a workmen's halt was provided on that line adjacent to the Bedlinog road and near the colliery entrance. Taff Merthyr Colliery Halt was brought into use during September 1927. It was a basic affair: the up platform, built of timber, was open to the elements, while the down platform was provided with a waiting shelter. Pathways on either side of a rail overbridge gave access to the platforms. The halt was supervised by the Bedlinog station master.

With both Deep Navigation and Taff Merthyr working to full capacity, the signalmen at Ocean Navigation box would have been busy men indeed. Apart from the passing general freight, coal traffic from other parts and the Pontypool Road—Aberdare—Neath passenger service, there were also the daily trains in and out of Deep Navigation and the Taff Merthyr branch. With the two colliery junctions only 21 chains apart it made economic sense to control them from one signal box

required to come to a stand on the viaduct and then set back into a siding at which point a colliery locomotive drew the empty wagons into the pit yard. Later, probably at or just after the acquisition of the colliery by the new owners, the signal box was renamed Ocean Navigation. It was equipped with a 21-lever frame and a block switch was provided. During the colliery's 'shutdown' — a local term used to describe the miners' annual holiday — the box was switched out.

A general view of Trelewis Halt looking east towards Nelson in June 1963. As is evident the halt was not provided with a footbridge but passengers alighting at the down platform were able to reach the Treharris road by means of a footpath at the far end. About eight passenger trains daily in both directions called at the halt and the shift porter — who can be seen strolling along the down platform — was a familiar sight supervising passengers over the crossing in the foreground. Supervision was necessary here as a good deal of colliery traffic trundled through the halt by day and by night. The competing bus and rail routes rubbed shoulders here: the main Nelson—Treharris—Bedlinog road is directly behind the iron railings and entrance gate on the left. (R. H. Marrows)

A postcard view of Treharris Viaduct long before its three arches were obliterated by colliery waste. The date of the photograph is unknown but is probably before the First World War. Traffic bound for Aberdare and Neath would have passed right to left in this view. The Taff Bargoed River flows — or in this summertime view trickles — through the central arch of the viaduct and through the single arch of the Cardiff Road bridge in the foreground. The winding gear of Deep Navigation Colliery can be seen on the extreme left. (D. L. Morgan Collection)

The terraced streets of Treharris and the buildings and winding gear of Deep Navigation Colliery provide the background to this April 1964 view of Ocean & Taff Merthyr Collieries signal box. In the foreground can be seen the gated Taff Merthyr branch. The wooden building behind the gate was used as a mess room by number-takers and shunters up until closure of the VoN to passenger traffic. At this location the VoN altered direction and curved through more than ninety degrees towards Treharris and Quaker's Yard. The viaduct is out of sight behind the trees on the left. Two months after this photograph was taken the signal box was taken out of use following closure of the VoN.
(R. H. Marrows)

---

from a more central position, rather than retain Ocean and establish a new box at the junction for Taff Merthyr.

On Sunday 24th July 1927 work was carried out to bring into use a new signal box to replace the original Ocean Navigation. The new box was positioned on the up side east of the viaduct, 237 yards from the old box. Although it was situated on a curve, the signalmen at the new Ocean and Taff Merthyr Collieries Signal Box were afforded good views of both colliery junctions. At this time the ground frame, from which the trailing connection from the up main to the Taff Merthyr Colliery Sidings had been worked, was taken out of use. Detonator-placer machines were fixed on both main running lines. Existing telephones and block instruments in Ocean Navigation box were transferred to the new box.

The new signal box was a standard GWR gable-end timber structure with a 39-lever vertical tappet frame. A block switch was provided. The box was interfaced with Nelson & Llancaiach to the east and Quaker's Yard East Junction to the west. The longest 'pull' was the up main advanced starter, situated on the up side, a distance of 555 yards. At opening, a pair of re-railing ramps was kept underneath the box.

Taff Merthyr Colliery sidings were laid a short distance from the junction with the VoN and for the subsequent 35 years the entrance to the branch was gated. To give the reader an insight into the method of working these sidings, and those at Deep Navigation, it is useful here to quote from the GWR (Newport Division) Notice No.268 which covered the bringing into use of the new signal box:

OCEAN NAVIGATION COLLIERY SIDINGS

Traffic detached or attached at these Sidings must be dealt with in precisely the same manner as at present, except that in the case of Engines requiring to run round their Vans or other traffic on the Main Lines this must be done between the two Crossover Roads in their new positions, and Drivers and Guards must arrange accordingly.

TAFF MERTHYR COLLIERY SIDINGS

The whole of the new Colliery Sidings are not yet completed, but the following sidings have been laid in and are available for use:

Sidings	Holding Capacity	To be used for
No.1	65 wagons	Inwards traffic
No.2	58 wagons	Outwards traffic
No.3	55 wagons	Outwards traffic
No.4	11 wagons	Cripple wagons

Until such time as the Colliery Sidings are completed the following arrangements must apply to trains detaching or attaching traffic at the sidings:

DOWN TRAINS

Down trains must be stopped at the Down Home signal, where empties or inwards traffic must be detached from the train and drawn down between the two crossover roads. The engine must then be uncoupled and run round the shunt, and be attached at the opposite end, subsequently drawing the wagons through the crossover to the Up Main line, and propelling them to the Colliery Sidings.

Traffic from the Colliery Sidings to be attached to Down trains must be dealt with vice-versa.

UP TRAINS

Traffic detached or attached by Up trains must be dealt with in the ordinary way through the trailing connection from the Up Main line to the Colliery Sidings.

A Shunter is employed at the Colliery Sidings, and he must keep in close touch with the Signalman in regard to trains calling to do work at the Sidings, and also with the Colliery Company's Staff with a view to obtaining prompt clearance of empties and Inwards traffic detached at the Sidings.

To round off this account of railway development in the area, it is worth mentioning that in 1934 the GWR opened Trelewis Halt four chains south of the junction for the Taff Merthyr branch. The siting of the halt was critical; with the growing threat of competition from local omnibus services very much in mind, the GWR positioned the halt within a few yards of the main thoroughfare that linked Bedlinog, Treharris and Nelson. The halt was equipped with a ticket office and waiting room on the up side and a corrugated zinc shelter on the down. The halt was manned permanently by a porter on each shift. For a small village, Trelewis was more than adequately served by railway as a few hundred yards away another station named Trelewis Platform, on the Taff Bargoed Joint line, had been opened to the public in 1911.

In 1954 the National Coal Board (NCB) opened Trelewis Drift, immediately north of Taff Merthyr. At its busiest it employed about 400 men who produced around 425,000 tons of dry steam coal annually. Towards the end of its working life, coal mined at the drift was blended with coal produced by Taff Merthyr. It is believed that shortly before closure poor quality coal was being extracted from the Drift and much of it

was considered unsuitable for power station use. As a result, some of the Drift's output did not find its way to Aberthaw Power station, but instead was taken by spoil train for dumping at Nelson East. British Coal closed Trelewis Drift in 1991.

Taff Merthyr was an all-electric pit but its locomotives until the 1960s were steam. It is not possible to present a comprehensive account of the pit's stud of locomotives but a selection is given here. Hudswell Clarke 0-6-0ST *Taff Merthyr* arrived at the colliery new in 1923 and was at work during development of the pit. The locomotive worked for 45 years before being scrapped in 1968. Andrew Barclay 0-4-0ST *Nelson* worked at the colliery but details of the engine's working life are not known. *Taff Merthyr No.3*, an Andrew Barclay 0-6-0ST, worked at the pit from 1955. The colliery itself was commemorated in 1982 when BR No.56 035 was named *Taff Merthyr* at a brief ceremony attended by Sir Peter Parker, the then chairman of British Rail.

Deep Navigation was renowned for its high-quality steam coal. Apart from house coal for domestic purposes, it was once a prime supplier to The Admiralty. It also supplied Aberthaw

On 25th March 1991 Class 37 No.37 696 is seen with a train of mgr hoppers being loaded with power station coal from Deep Navigation Colliery, Treharris, at Ocean. The locomotive is standing near the junction for the Taff Merthyr branch and the train is straddling Treharris Viaduct. Close inspection of the photograph will show the south parapet of the viaduct and the tops of the arches which are just visible above the colliery waste which for years had been spread out on the site and which eventually almost totally engulfed the structure. The village of Trelewis is in the background and the modern footbridge, extreme top left, marks the course of the Taff Bargoed line to Cwmbargoed. (R. H. Marrows)

power station and in later years the power station at Didcot. Trainloads to the latter place in recent years were, at times, interesting in that a single wagon was attached to the rear of a merry-go-round train. The wagon, bearing the initials 'GW', carried a supply of loco coal to the Great Western Society at Didcot. The colliery also provided the loco coal for Abercynon mpd before and during the Second World War.

GWR and BR locomotives worked as far as the sidings on the up side at Deep Navigation, after which empties were taken into the colliery for loading and brought back out to the sidings by the colliery's engines. Colliery fitters maintained the pit's two steam locomotives during the course of their daily work. It is interesting to point out here that when steam was replaced by diesel for shunting around the cramped colliery yard, the fitters continued to maintain the new machines by trial and error even though they received no formal training in the repair and maintenance of the new form of motive power.

On 13th June 1964 the VoN closed as a through route. On this date Ocean & Taff Merthyr Collieries signal box was closed although it stood for another twenty years serving a useful purpose as a mess room and refuge in inclement weather for the hardy shunters who supervised the arrival and departure of coal traffic.

The word 'Ocean' was in general use for many years to describe the area in which the Deep Navigation traffic, and the traffic from Taff Merthyr, converged. As with other selected locations along the entire VoN, a section survived at Treharris exclusively for colliery traffic. Stopblocks were installed at the end of a headshunt east of Treharris station. Traffic from both collieries reached Ystrad Mynach via the surviving two and a half mile stretch of the VoN as far as Penallta Junction and the one and a half mile Penallta branch.

The Type 3 diesels, later Class 37, made their first appearances in 1964, at first sharing duties with steam. By the end of that year, the ex-GWR '56XX' Class 0-6-2Ts and other assorted Great Western classes that had laboured on coal traffic had made their final bow after which all traffic to Ocean was in the capable charge of the new diesel locomotives. A

number of classes appeared at Ocean, but generally it was the reliable Class 37 that did the bulk of the work.

Until September 1968 Nelson & Llancaiach signal box controlled traffic to the two collieries as it did the coal and foundry traffic along the Taff Bargoed to Cwmbargoed and Dowlais. Following closure of Nelson box, control of both lines passed to Ystrad Mynach South.

At Taff Merthyr traffic to and from the colliery was hauled along the branch by the colliery engines working as far as Taff Merthyr Colliery Sidings. With the introduction of mgr trains, BR locomotives worked along the branch and into the colliery complex. A 2mph speed limit was observed as a rake of hoppers was drawn through the colliery's conveyor-assisted loading mechanism. Using the colliery's new conveyor and bunker loading facilities, it was possible to load an mgr train in twenty minutes. A pair of Class 37s double-heading 36 hopper wagons was a familiar sight at Taff Merthyr during the 1970s through to the early 1990s.

After one hundred years of mining at Deep Navigation, almost all available space that had been used for tipping colliery waste had been exhausted. Such was the quantity of waste tipped and spread over the area of land east of the

---

Class 37 No.37 699 brings a train of empties onto the Taff Merthyr branch in October 1992. Although out of sight, the tail of the train is passing the location of Trelewis Halt. During the early diesel period a ground frame controlled traffic on to the branch but in later years points were hand-operated. At the time of this photograph, a signalman's agent was housed in a Portacabin at Nelson, where the Ocean and Cwmbargoed lines diverged. The agent worked in conjunction with the signalman at Ystrad Mynach and a chargeman or shunter at Ocean. A staff marked 'Nelson—Taff Merthyr' was issued to the driver of a train proceeding to Taff Merthyr Colliery. (R. H. Marrows)

Deep Navigation Colliery ceased production on Good Friday, 29th March 1991. A few weeks before closure, Class 37 No.37 799 is seen passing the colliery with a train of empties, prior to running round and returning to the loading point on Treharris Viaduct. At this location the train is on a gently rising gradient and is running towards the site of Treharris station. Note the milepost on the right – 14¾ miles from Pontypool Road. (R. H. Marrows)

colliery that, as the years passed, the arches of the viaduct were filled in, to such an extent that only the parapets of the structure could be seen. To the stranger it appeared as if a wall had been built on the spoil tip. It is a fact, locally, that many of the younger population of the district did not realise that a viaduct existed at all!

Close inspection of the accompanying location map will show a single line linking the Taff Merthyr branch with Deep Navigation colliery yard. This line, nine chains in length, was brought into use in 1978. The exact reason for its existence is not known but it may well have been put in for the exchange of wagons between collieries. It is also highly unlikely that BR locomotives were allowed to run upon it. Until mechanical loading was established near (and on) the viaduct, BR locomotives were allowed as far as a warning board at Deep Navigation.

With Deep Navigation Colliery in the background, an unidentified Class 37 and a train of empties gingerly negotiates the tight curves of the Taff Merthyr branch. Note the vast amount of waste spread on the adjoining colliery ground. Mgr trains continued to travel along the branch until the closure of Taff Merthyr Colliery in June 1993. (R. H. Marrows)

To remedy the tipping problem, the NCB established a discharge point at Nelson East Siding — often referred to as 'Nelson Bog' — on the site of Penalltau Junction. The latter had been the location at which the Rhymney Railway's Penalltau branch had dropped away from the VoN down to Ystrad Mynach and the Cardiff—Rhymney main line. The siding was brought into use in September 1977.

For a period during the 1980s, coal mined at Deep Navigation and Taff Merthyr was taken to Cwmbargoed for blending. These heavy trains were topped and tailed by Class 37s and were required to reverse at Nelson for the continuous seven-mile ascent at full throttle to Cwmbargoed on the bleak Dowlais Moor.

Looking up the valley towards Taff Merthyr Colliery in March 1991, Class 37 No.37 691 with a trainload of pit waste bound for the discharge point at Nelson East. Taff Merthyr Colliery can be seen through the trees in the right background. At this location the scenery is pleasantly rural and, although out of site, the Taff Bargoed River runs between the trees and the ancient waste heaps behind the train. (R. H. Marrows)

By 1990 Barry depot was responsible for about twenty daily mgr workings to South Wales collieries, including Deep Navigation and Taff Merthyr. Without access to official records it is difficult to state with accuracy the number of trains per day working to and from Ocean during the diesel era. In the late 1980s there were three or four loaded mgrs daily from Deep Navigation and the same number from Taff Merthyr. During September 1990 extra trains were required to cope with a brief but impressive surge in production at Taff Merthyr. During that month, following a particularly productive week a Welsh mining record was set up when over 40,000 tons of coal was produced in the B24 Retreat face.

On 29th March 1991, after 112 years of mining, Deep Navigation was closed by British Coal. At closure 371 men were employed at the pit. The removal of the coal stocks continued for a few months. Taff Merthyr suffered the same fate two years later, the final shift being worked on 11th June 1993.

Today, little remains of the VoN in Treharris or of the two collieries for that matter. Much of the trackbed has been converted to a cycle path. Landscaping has obliterated the site of Trelewis Halt and both colliery junctions. The demolition of

Treharris Viaduct caused concern amongst some older members of the public, particularly those with a sense of history. With a little ingenuity the handsome 140-year-old structure could easily have been incorporated attractively into the landscape. Ocean provided miners and railwaymen with 120 years of useful employment in a location which was full of industrial history. It is ironic that even that comparatively modern form of railway traction — the workhorse Class 37 diesel locomotive — is now part of that history.

Taff Merthyr Colliery, 21st October 1991. In this view looking south, Class 37 No.37 798 has brought a train of hoppers to the north end of the colliery, before running round and taking the train through the loading apparatus. The Taff Bargoed River, which was diverted when the colliery was developed, can be seen on the right. The line to Cwmbargoed runs at a higher level and is just below the road in the left middle background. (R. H. Marrows)

6

Taff Bargoed Pictorial

Steam and Diesel between Nelson and Dowlais

The Taff Bargoed Joint Railway (GWR/Rhymney Railway) was brought into use in 1876 as a means of transporting iron ore to the Dowlais Works. It was double line from the start and the gradients were amongst the fiercest in South Wales. A passenger service was introduced on 1st February 1876. At first trains left Llancaiach on the Vale of Neath line for the 9½-mile journey to the terminus at Dowlais (Cae Harris). In this view, taken on the 6th June 1963, a Dowlais train can be seen in the branch platform at Nelson and Llancaiach, which was opened in 1912 to replace Llancaiach. The latter station was about one hundred yards to the east beyond the station footbridge. (R. H. Marrows)

In 1965 the Taff Bargoed was singled. In this October 1992 view, Class 37 No.37 796 is seen passing Nelson with a train of empty mgr wagons from Aberthaw to Cwmbargoed. Even this comparatively modern scene has changed with the line in the foreground to Ocean (for Deep Navigation and Taff Merthyr collieries) having been lifted, added to which the Taff Bargoed line was realigned to pass beneath the right-hand span of the bridge. From this point the seven miles to Cwmbargoed is on a continuous rising gradient with the steepest at 1 in 40. The line sees little or no use these days and its future depends very much on Cwmbargoed's survival as a railhead. (R. H. Marrows)

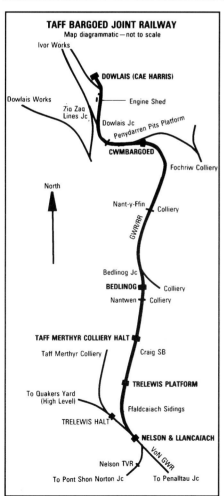

TAFF BARGOED JOINT RAILWAY
Map diagrammatic—not to scale

Ivor Works

DOWLAIS (CAE HARRIS)

Dowlais Works

Engine Shed

Zig Zag
Lines Jc.

Dowlais Jc

Penydarren Pits Platform

CWMBARGOED

Fochriw Colliery

North

Nant-y-Ffin — Colliery

GWR/RR

Bedlinog Jc

BEDLINOG — Colliery

Nantwen — Colliery

TAFF MERTHYR COLLIERY HALT

Taff Merthyr Colliery

Craig SB

TRELEWIS PLATFORM

To Quakers Yard
(High Level)

Ffaldcaiach Sidings

TRELEWIS HALT

NELSON & LLANCAIACH

VoN GWR

Nelson TVR

To Pont Shon Norton Jc   To Penalltau Jc

In 1964 No.D6820 waits at Ffaldcaiach with a train of empty wagons. The driver of the diesel locomotive is waiting for two reasons: first, for a '56XX' Class 0-6-2T to provide banking assistance, and secondly, for a pilotman as telegraph lines had been stolen! The banking engine, of Cae Harris shed, is out of sight around the curve in the background. (R. H. Marrows)

In the up direction, the first stopping place was Trelewis Platform which was brought into public use in 1911. In this late summer 1964 view looking north towards Bedlinog, an English Electric Type 3 (Class 37) hauls empty mineral wagons to Cwmbargoed, banked by an ex-GWR '56XX' Class 0-6-2T of Cae Harris shed. The passenger service between Nelson and Dowlais had been withdrawn a few months earlier on 13th June. Note the weed-clogged and rusting up line which had been out of use since the early 1950s, following a landslip above Taff Merthyr Colliery. From that time on, single line working had been established between Ffaldcaiach and Bedlinog. (R. H. Marrows)

On 10th June 2000 privately-owned Class '37' No.37 038 with six coaches (including a buffet car) approaches Trelewis with a return working of a Valley Lines Special from Cardiff to Cwmbargoed. Taff Merthyr Garden Village can be seen on the hillside. Although not visible in this view, the alignment of the short branch to Taff Merthyr Colliery ran at a lower level through the trees in the foreground. (R. H. Marrows)

LEFT: On 17th March 1993, a pair of Class 37s with a train of empty mgr wagons for Cwmbargoed is seen passing the site of Taff Merthyr Colliery Halt. At a lower level near the river, the colliery is coming to the end of its working life. Three months later, on 11th June, the final shift was worked. The winding gear and mgr bunker was demolished by explosion on 22nd July 1994. In the right upper background the line of trees indicates the route of the line to Cwmbargoed. The village of Bedlinog can be seen on the hillside.
(R. H. Marrows)

Along with Cwmbargoed, Bedlinog was an original intermediate station on the Taff Bargoed. Although centrally situated, the station itself occupied a site halfway up one of the steepest thoroughfares in South Wales. On 26th September 1960 ex-GWR '56XX' Class 0-6-2T No.5603 is about to leave Bedlinog with the 2.41p.m. train from Nelson to Dowlais (Cae Harris). The booking office was at road level and as can be seen, by its very appearance, was occasionally mistaken for a signal box! (HCC/RMC)

LEFT: At Bedlinog Junction, a short distance north of Bedlinog station, a branch ran off to Bedlinog Colliery which stood on levelled ground above the village. This colliery closed in 1924, but a level was worked there until the 1950s. In August 1964 an ex-GWR '56XX' Class 0-6-2T and 'Toad' brake van are seen near the junction. The remains of the staggered platforms of Bedlinog Colliers' Platform are out of sight in the cutting to the right. (R. H. Marrows)

The head of the Taff Bargoed Valley as seen from a carriage window on a train from Dowlais (Cae Harris) to Ystrad Mynach. Having just passed the up distant signal, ex-GWR '56XX' Class 0-6-2T No.5603 is seen approaching Cwmbargoed with a train of empties for Dowlais on 10th July 1958. (HCC/RMC)

Dowlais (Cae Harris), 11th April 1964. Ex-GWR '56XX' Class 0-6-2T No.5677 is in the process of running-round its two coaches, after which it will propel them into the platform. (R. H. Marrows)

A general view of the station and arrival/departure platform at Dowlais (Cae Harris), 28th December 1963. As can be seen there was no engine release available. (R. H. Marrows)

BELOW: *Three '56XX' Class 0-6-2Ts can be seen on shed at Cae Harris on 28th December 1963. The main line runs between the signal box and the shed and curves sharply away to the right towards Cwmbargoed. Cae Harris shed closed to steam at the end of 1964 after which it was used — minus its roof — for overnight stabling of diesel locomotives.* (R. H. Marrows)

Someone once wrote that the station building at Dowlais (Cae Harris) had a distinctly 'ecclesiastical' look. This is a view taken on 17th April 1965 with the photographer's back to High Street. The passenger service had been withdrawn ten months earlier and some of the building's fittings have been removed. Cae Harris signal box is still in place in the background.
(R. H. Marrows)

The date is 31st July 1965 and the Monmouthshire Railway Society's 'Rambling 56' has come to a stand at Dowlais (Cae Harris). The train, hauled by smartly turned-out GWR '56XX' Class 0-6-2T No.6643, was unable to proceed any further as the platform line had been lifted. Note the photographer on one of Dowlais' many famous waste-heaps. (R. H. Marrows)

7

Adventures at Radyr Junction

The working life of a shunter

At first acquaintance well-heeled Radyr, in north west Cardiff, seems an unlikely place as the location of an extensive railway installation. It is, in fact, out of sight from the main thoroughfare of Heol Isaf. A left turn when driving south takes one along Station Road, a busy place edged by a parade of shops. Suddenly the road narrows and becomes a leafy lane, dropping steeply down to the park and ride station which is today's Radyr. To the south of the recently remodelled station and on the up side stands the new Valleys Radyr signalling centre. This takes the form of a couple of single-storey, almost windowless grey buildings with a perimeter fence of spiked steel, which now controls the ex-Taff Vale Railway main line from Cardiff as far as Abercynon and the branch from Pontypridd to Treherbert.

All trace of the semaphore signals that were an attractive feature of Radyr has disappeared following the resignalling scheme which was completed a few years ago. In the immediate area three mechanical boxes closed. These were at Radyr Junction, Radyr Quarry and Llandaff Loop and, except

In September 1963 GWR '56XX' Class 0-6-2T No.5654 is seen passing the gantry at Radyr with a coal train on the down relief line. Radyr Junction signal box can be seen in the background. This British Railways box was brought into use in 1961, replacing a TVR structure which stood on the same side a few yards to the south. Note the booking office, referred to in the text, on the down platform. (R. H. Marrows)

RADYR

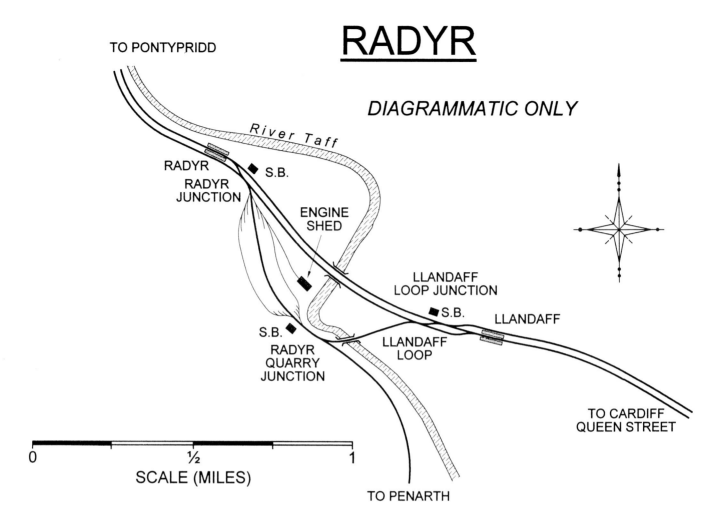

DIAGRAMMATIC ONLY

TO PONTYPRIDD

River Taff

RADYR
RADYR
JUNCTION

S.B.

ENGINE
SHED

LLANDAFF
LOOP JUNCTION

S.B.

LLANDAFF

S.B.
RADYR
QUARRY
JUNCTION

LLANDAFF
LOOP

TO CARDIFF
QUEEN STREET

0   ½   1

SCALE (MILES)

TO PENARTH

for a retaining wall cut into an embankment where the latter box stood, it is as if those boxes never existed in the first place. All trace of them has been swept away.

South of Radyr station the main line continues to Cardiff Queen Street. Immediately beyond the platform slopes the City Line turns south west to reach Cardiff Central, via Danescourt and Ninian Park. In the vee of this junction there is a vast expanse of land which today is a wilderness of weeds, saplings and the odd forgotten rusting rail. Part of this piece of land is in the process of being cleared for building purposes. This was the site of Radyr Junction yard, a location once synonymous with freight-handling in south east Wales. That which follows are the recollections of a shunter employed when Radyr Junction was busy, through to its gradual rundown, which coincided with the decline and almost total destruction of the South Wales coal industry.

But first a few notes on Radyr are necessary here to set the scene, so to speak, to provide the background for what was a strategic location on the railway map of south east Wales. The Taff Vale main line from Cardiff to Merthyr was opened throughout in 1841. Traffic had begun running in 1840 but only as far as Navigation House (later Abercynon). The Penarth Railway was brought into use in 1859. This line

branched away from the main line at Radyr to the south west and sidings were laid near the junction the following year. Radyr station was opened in 1863 and the original TVR two-road engine shed stood at the south end of the station.

In 1900 the double-line Llandaff Loop was brought into use. Study of the accompanying map will show that the loop provided traffic with a southern entrance to, or exit from, the yard. The loop, which crossed the River Taff by means of a viaduct, was controlled by Radyr Quarry and Llandaff Loop signal boxes.

In 1931 the GWR provided a new shed as a replacement for the old TVR depot. Radyr was originally a sub-shed to Cardiff (Cathays). In December 1957 it was allocated code 88A following the closure of Cathays. Many of the locomotives from the latter were transferred to Radyr. Radyr Junction was responsible for something like 25 mineral and goods workings which were identifiable by the target letter 'Y' together with the relevant number. There were other workings which did not carry a target such as a Monday Only Radyr Quarry Junction to Salisbury and Radyr Quarry Junction to Severn Tunnel Junction. The shed was re-coded 88B on 1st June 1961 and it finally closed to steam in July 1965. The foregoing gives only the briefest account of Radyr Junction. For a greater

The extent of Radyr yard is shown looking south and as viewed from the landing of a floodlight pylon. The date is 2nd June 1982 when special trains were run to Cardiff bringing people to the city to witness the visit of Pope John Paul. A number of these trains ran empty stock from Ninian Park to Radyr. Two of these trains can be seen: a Class 47 stands on the up branch and alongside another is headed by a Class 37. Other coaching stock can be seen in the adjoining sidings. The pre-assembly plant is on the extreme left. (Wayne Evans)

---

understanding of its history — dates, traffic, etc — readers are advised to refer to the bibliography.

I now move on to the late 1960s by which time steam had vanished, the diesel locomotive reigned supreme and the yard still had plenty of traffic, providing work for 200 men of various occupations and grades. The recollections that follow are those of Mr. Joel V. Morris who related them to me enthusiastically and with a considerable amount of detail. I therefore decided that it was far better to let him have his head, rather than 'ghost' his story using my own words, hence the use of quotes for reported speech. I have dabbled very little with what he related to me during the course of three lengthy interviews, but I have taken the liberty of arranging matters in some kind of chronological order and adding some technical and historical detail here and there. This is Mr. Morris's story:

"I suppose I was an average pupil and when it was time for me to leave school in Aberfan in 1967 I had no real idea of what I wanted to do. My father, a tough, uncompromising man who was a boxer in his youth, asked me if I would like a job on the railway. He was a goods guard at Abercynon and felt able to use his influence to get me started although he had no particular job in mind.

"But I went my own way and got a job in a factory. I earned £6 a week and it was awful. I spent four months at this job but eventually packed it in. Around this time they were advertising for recruits into the mining industry so I applied and was accepted as a trainee at the National Coal Board training centre at Aberaman. We were taught pit safety and various aspects of the mining industry. We visited local collieries to learn how coal was mined and brought to the surface. I recall one instructor taking us to a new face and inviting me to pull out a piece of coal. As I held the lump in my hands he told me that I was the first human being to touch that particular piece and that it was millions of years old. This remark impressed me but for some reason I could not take to the idea of mining as a way of making a living. So I handed in my notice and decided to try something else. My dear late mother's words had come back to haunt me as I can remember her saying that 'No son of mine is working in the pits!'

"On hearing of my failed attempt at a career in mining, my father in his usual straightforward and direct manner asked me again: 'Are you ready for a start on the railway now, boy?' I replied that I was and he fixed it for me to attend an interview at Radyr.

"In 1969 at the age of 17 I became a railwayman at Radyr Junction and the job I undertook was that of a messenger boy. I went to Marland House, Cardiff, for a medical examination and the railway doctor declared that I was fit for every kind of railway work. I was then given a railway uniform. These came in two sizes – too small and too big!

"My duties as a messenger boy were routine but one duty that was considered a priority was delivering the weekly notices to signal boxes. These notices informed signalmen of engineering work, speed restrictions and changes to rules. I was paid £17 a week. This job entailed a lot of walking alongside the track and in places designated for walking. I was warned that I had to be vigilant at all times owing to the amount of traffic in and out of the yard and the passenger traffic up and down the main line. I visited three boxes during the course of my rounds. These were Radyr Junction, Radyr Quarry Junction and Llandaff Loop. Little did I realise at the time that 25 years later I would become very well acquainted

In March 1993, during the final days of Radyr, Class 31 No.31 105 is seen leaving Radyr yard with an Engineering Department working to Bescot. The Llandaff Loop can be seen branching away to the right and in the background is Radyr Quarry Junction signal box. (R. H. Marrows)

In March 1993 shunter No.09 015 is about to leave the yard with an assortment of vehicles on a trip working to Cathays. Radyr Quarry Junction signal box, in the background, remained in use for a further five years. The box was brought into use in 1900 but missed its centenary by two years, being taken out of use in 1998. (R. H. Marrows)

Radyr Junction looking north towards the station on 2nd June 1982. In this view taken from a floodlight pylon, a Class 37 is propelling the empty stock of an excursion into the up relief line on the day of the Pope's visit to Cardiff. The Cardiff—Merthyr line is to the right and alongside is Radyr Junction signal box. (Wayne Evans)

with these three boxes, all of which were within a reasonably easy walk of Radyr. I was also required to take weekly notices to Walnut Tree signal box at Taffs Well. During that first year of railway work I spent a lot of time walking.

"I wasn't long getting into the swing of railway work and found the other men a fairly friendly bunch. Some of the Cardiffians referred to me as 'Taff' which is unusual in South Wales as it is rare for a Welshman to refer to another Welshman as 'Taff'. They probably called me this because I was a valley boy and most of those working at Radyr were from in or around Cardiff. I got to know people quickly and it was not unusual when I was delivering notices to the boxes for the signalmen to have a cup of tea ready. I was enjoying the work and all the time Radyr was busy 24 hours a day. Another of my duties was taking the log book of movements to the Yardmaster for his approval and inspection. He inhabited an office which I think was an old signal box in the vee of the junction. I can't remember his name, but he was the big chief and he insisted on the log book being on his desk ready for him before he got in.

"My time as a messenger boy lasted about a year. One day, a friend of mine who was a porter at Llandaff, rang me up and tipped me off that there was a vacancy for a porter at Radyr station. I applied for the job and got it. Portering duties were straightforward, such as keeping the platform swept clean and assisting passengers and making sure doors were secure before departure. From time to time I booked tickets. In those days Radyr had a typical booking office with a small window through which communication was made with passengers. On the desk by the window was an Edmondson ticket dating machine and affixed to the walls were racks of pre-printed card tickets. Work in the office was routine and consisted mainly of the issue of tickets for commuters to Cardiff and up the valleys to Pontypridd, Treherbert and Merthyr. I can remember only once having to write a ticket and that was a rail warrant for a soldier returning to camp. Daily takings were placed in a leather pouch which was placed in the travelling safe, a big sturdy square box with a one-way flap. The safe was put on a passenger train to Cardiff.

"But one day I did something that I was sure would get me the sack. It was about 8.15 in the morning and I wasn't particularly busy. A young man came into the ticket office. He looked a bit concerned and was in a state of agitation. The trouble was he had left his home in a hurry and had arrived at the station and suddenly discovered that he had forgotten his wallet and had no money, not even loose change. He explained his situation to me and asked if I could possibly let him have a return to Cardiff, which cost 1s 9d (9p), and he would pay

me the amount back the following morning. He added that he had to be in Cardiff by nine o'clock and that he did not have time to return home for his money.

"I thought for a moment and weighed the man up. He was well-spoken, nicely-dressed in a dark suit and carried a briefcase and I could see he was in a bit of a state. To me he looked genuine. So I let him have a return to Cardiff for which he thanked me. Now, I was responsible for seeing that when a ticket was sold I received the right money. So, to keep accounts in order I took 1s 9d from the office float and put it with the rest of the day's takings. There was always a £2 float kept in the office. What I had done was wrong but I trusted the man and thought no more of it.

"But an hour later I became worried because as my bad luck would have it, the district auditor turned up as part of his routine of checking station accounts and on that day, of all days, I had taken it upon myself the break the rules. I became a bag of nerves as he went through the books and checked the takings. He noticed the 1s 9d missing from the float and I explained to him what had happened and that the passenger had promised to pay the following day. The auditor's face reddened and he informed me that what I had done was 'highly irregular'. He left the office and I saw no more of him for the remainder of my shift.

"The following morning the auditor returned and sat in the office while I issued a few tickets. The man returned as promised and repaid the 1s 9d which he owed and he also bought a ticket. The man could see I appeared a bit worried

and he must have seen the grim-faced auditor sat in a chair behind me. I'm sure the man had got wind of my problem so he rubbed in his thanks to me for being helpful and declared that I had provided a good example of 'public relations'. The money had been paid, the books balanced and everyone was happy. The auditor saw and heard all of this but said nothing to me. He left the office without so much as a good morning — and I never saw him again. But I have often wondered what would have happened to me had the man not returned to pay me for the ticket I had given him the day before.

"After twelve months of portering I moved on to do a stint as a lampman which once again was a job which meant a lot of walking. After a few weeks of basic instruction by one of the older men on how to trim wicks and fill lamps, I was allotted my own patch which consisted of Radyr Junction, Radyr Quarry, Llandaff Loop, Dock Storage North and at Heath Halt (Low Level) on the Coryton Branch. There was plenty of work to keep me occupied as there were semaphore signals and ground discs everywhere, especially at Radyr. I carried a long stick which was notched so that the lamps could be carried safely.

"I had two distants at the north end of Radyr station, not far from Gelynis Crossing. One was sited for the down relief and the other for the down main. Radyr was so busy with freight that it was safer for me to walk along the up main than the relief when I was making for these two signals.

"There was a big gantry at Radyr station which had an array of signals. I can tell you that I've been on that gantry during the course of lamping duties and the boards, for the down main and for the yard, were forever going on and off. There was also a signalman at Radyr Quarry who never let me forget that he was on duty by 'wiggling' a signal as I replaced a lamp. With all the work involved in lamping around Radyr I had to be careful because of the huge amount of traffic — and there were no high-visibility vests then.

"Having worked as a messenger boy, porter and lampman, I think I had received a good grounding as a railwayman. It was essential to be familiar with the rule book and to work safely. But it was time to move on after lamping for about a year. I fancied a change and through the vacancy list I discovered there was a vacancy for a shunter in Radyr yard. I applied for the job and was accepted. Shunters' jobs were graded and I

An undated view of Class 37 No.37 704 on a Tower Colliery—Aberthaw Power Station mgr train passing Radyr Quarry. The building to the right was the Radyr Quarry foreman's cabin. (R. H. Marrows)

started as the Radyr Quarry foreman's mate — the third man as I was known. I worked under his orders.

"The pecking order in the world of the shunter was yard supervisor, yard foreman, head shunter, under shunter and third man. I normally worked with the same group of people. There were 25 shunters at Radyr. Even in the early 1970s the railway was still a big employer and every train in and out of the yard had a second man in the cab and a guard. The first implement to which I was introduced was the shunter's pole which was light and pliable, about six feet long with a metal hook at the far end. I soon got used to the pole and perfected the way of catching a link with the hook and flicking it on to the drawgear of the wagon. It may sound a bit silly, but to this day I do not know what wood the pole was made from and I used one for many years.

"Radyr yard was in three sections with 30 roads. These were numbered as follows: 1-8 Bog, 9-18 Goods, 19-30 New Section. New 27, 28, 29 and Goods 16, 17, 18 were stop block roads. Number 30 was the shed road. The old four-road steam shed was used for cleaning Powell-Duffryn tanks. The yard

Shortly before closure, No. 09 015 acting as yard pilot, is signalled into the S&T sidings on the up side of Radyr yard. Radyr Junction signal box in the background was of British Railways origin with its frame facing the back wall and, as with Radyr Quarry and Llandaff Loop boxes, remained in use until 1998. (R. H. Marrows)

was floodlit and had a Tannoy system to aid communication generally. It was rare to see an empty road at Radyr. One siding was kept empty for a train to arrive and another was kept empty so that a new train could be formed if at all possible. There was also a Pre-Assembly Depot at Radyr. This was where track sections and pointwork were assembled. In my early days it was certainly a busy place. On afternoon shift there would be trains nose to tail on the down relief from Walnut Tree all the way to the gantry at Radyr. This would be a distance of about two miles and as they were all mixed traffic of coal, coke, duff and other bits and pieces a busy shift was in prospect.

"A shift would begin by our gang assembling in our cabin where the head shunter and foreman would plan the work for the first couple of hours. A slateboard, marked off into squares, was kept in the cabin. It gave us a visual indication of what traffic we had in each siding, for example: 1 Bog, 30 Scunthorpes; 9 Goods, 60 mixed; 21 New, 35 Swansea. The board also reminded us how many wagons each siding would hold. Yes, it was old-fashioned, but it worked. When a train had been formed and despatched, its details were wiped from

the board but recorded in a log book. Once these trains were formed and despatched, the next trains were marshalled. There was enough work to keep us occupied for a complete shift. I can tell you that when a shift was finished we'd all done a good day's work. There was no hanging about as trains had to be ready for departure at a specified time.

"In a busy yard it is pointless trying to communicate by shouting to the drivers or other colleagues because of the noise from wagons being shunted and trains being formed. So we used hand signals. For instance, arms crossed in front of the head meant to the driver that his train was standing clear in a siding and not fouling another line. Pumping left fist upward was an instruction to a driver to create vacuum after we had connected the vacuum pipes on the wagons and the pipe to the engine. Flicking the hand forward meant pull away and flicking the hand backwards meant come towards me. The arm outstretched and waved up and down was the way of advising a driver to slow down. Straight arm held up meant prepare to stop. And the signal hand to mouth meant a cup of tea!

"At night hand signals weren't used as they couldn't be seen anyway. This is where the lamps came into use. Red light, stop. Green light meant all right to pull away. An amber light waved across the chest was an indication to slow down. The instruction for a driver to create vacuum was indicated by showing a red light which was moved up and down vertically.

"Funny and ridiculous things could happen, too. I think our foreman must have had a brainstorm. It was something I found difficult to understand from a man of many years' experience but I'll tell you all the same. We once formed a train of Actons (London). There were 44 wagons making 1,400 tons when we received a message from control of an additional load which 'must be on the Acton'. The additional load was a dead Class 47 loco which had to be marshalled next to the live loco.

_____

Steam and diesel at Radyr Junction in September 1963. In this view looking south, a six-car 'speed-whiskered' DMU has just left Radyr station and is travelling on the down main towards Llandaff and Cardiff Queen Street. Waiting at the signal to the right is an unidentified 0-6-0PT. The building with the tall chimney to the right was the abode of the yardmaster referred to in the text. (R. H. Marrows)

Therefore, we had to reduce the weight of the train. We worked out the weight of the dead loco at about 150 tons which was the equivalent of five hopper wagons at 30 tons each. So we decided that by removing five wagons from the train the dead loco could be accommodated bearing in mind we had to consider the total weight of the train. Job done, or so we thought. That is, until the foreman had a good idea.

"He thought that because we had two locomotives we could take double the load. We looked at him in bewilderment. The load for the train was 1,400 tons and he wanted to increase it to 2,800 tons! We tried to explain to him the error of his ways but for ten minutes his idea was king until one of my colleagues literally dumped him in a puddle. This seemed to bring him to his senses and he realised how silly his suggestion had been. It did not seem to dawn on him that the second loco was dead and that the weight of the train could not be increased. I think for a few minutes he had taken leave of his senses. He kept very quiet for the rest of the shift.

"During my time at Radyr odd things happened and one incident comes to mind. We had a 'Western' in one Saturday to hook up to an Acton. As the loco gently ran down a siding

to couple up to its train, it derailed for no apparent reason. The front bogie had come off. There was a lot of head-scratching but we weren't sure why the engine had come off the road. They brought a crane up from Canton to re-rail it and there was no damage done to the loco. But strange as it may seem, the following Saturday the same thing happened. The same loco derailed at the same spot. This seemed to me and my colleagues as no mere coincidence. In this particular siding where the engine had derailed, a nasty lump was discovered in one of the rails. Yard sidings are not noted for the excellence of their track but a locomotive travelling slowly was never known to de-rail, except in this case — and twice in the very same place. And then someone spotted it. One of the wheels on the loco's leading bogie had slight damage, it had become pitted in a very small area. It so happened that when the wheel turned, by a million to one chance, the damaged part of the wheel met the bump in the track and this is what caused the derailment. And this happened twice.

"I worked three shifts: days, afternoons and nights. The first few months were hard work. Every part of my body ached — shoulders, arms and legs. But once I had got into the job and had a fuller understanding of what was needed I became used to the physical side of it. By the end of four months I had never felt so fit. It was a job that kept me fit and kept me on my toes. Safety was paramount in such a busy yard; it was full of obstacles like hand-operated point levers. Great care had to be taken when crossing a siding where some wagons may have been stabled. It was brain-washed into me that when passing from one side to the other behind a wagon that I should walk ten feet beyond the wagon away from the buffers and then cross the line. I always gave a wagon a wide berth. You can imagine what would happen if a shunter crossed immediately behind a wagon and it was bumped during a shunting movement from the other end. To the best of my knowledge I cannot recall accidents in the yard during my time. Section J of the Rule Book covered the basic rules of shunting.

"It was mostly coal traffic that we handled and the destinations to which it was bound were Severn Tunnel Junction, Margam, Swansea Docks, Acton, West Drayton, Temple Mills, Scunthorpe, Stoke and Hawarden Bridge. There was also traffic in from Caerphilly Tar Plant and from Aberdare. Each wagon had a ticket fitted to the sole bar with the destination clearly marked and when forming trains weight and route availability had to be considered.

"We had six 08 Class 0-6-0 diesel shunters. Three of them worked in the yard and the other three undertook trip workings to such places as Cathays where damaged wagons were moved, and to Pontypridd Goods. When not required the Class 08 shunters were stored on the van road. There were no refuelling facilities in the yard which meant the locos ran to Canton, usually at the weekend, for refuelling and servicing. I can also remember a Ruston & Hornsby 165bhp diesel-electric working in the yard. Most of the locos were Canton engines, the Type 3 English Electric diesel, later known as Class 37. I occasionally saw a few of the diesel-hydraulic 'Westerns' at Radyr. These were impressive, handsome engines and two regulars come to mind — Nos.1020 *Western Hero* and 1010 *Western Campaigner.*

"There was a good spirit when marshalling a train. There was never a shunter's truck at Radyr, at least not that I can remember. We used to travel on the step of the loco. We had to work briskly and make sure a train was ready to be at the yard signal at a specified time. As an example I can tell you that a train for, say, Acton was formed in a set way. We knew it as station formation. Acton vacuum-fitted wagons were marshalled next to the engine with non-fitted next to the van. Temple Mills fitted were put behind the Acton fitted and the West Drayton non-fitted in front of the Acton non-fitted, if you see what I mean. A train such as this would weigh about 1,400 tons and the Acton was usually hauled by a Class 47, though on a Saturday it was worked for a period by a 'Western'.

"Saturday mornings were busy. This was the day when we formed four or five engineering trains for ballasting, relaying and bridge inspections and repairs. We were responsible for forming the engineering train when work in Caerphilly tunnel was planned. The engineering department always insisted that the train was formed exactly as they specified with a brake van at both ends, with mess vans and tool wagons in certain positions; the following week they'd want them in a different order! Some of the trains for Caerphilly Tunnel included Grampus wagons with tressles inside so that cement could be mixed for repairs to the tunnel roof, while there were tanks included in the train so that the tunnel walls could be washed. These trains usually consisted of 40 wagons in total and took about two hours to form.

"One day I spotted something that earned me a feather in my cap, or so I thought. We were forming a train and a few wagons were being shunted slowly towards me so that I could hook up to a brake van. As they approached me I noticed that one of the wagons wasn't running smoothly. It appeared to be rising on one corner in regular fashion as the wheel turned. I had to look hard because I thought I was seeing things as the wagon gently rose and dropped. Then I noticed that the wagon had a bent axle.

"I called the wagon examiner, Harry House, a giant of a man at six feet six inches, who came along and inspected the wagon. After a minute or so he issued the customary red card for the wagon 'Not to be Moved'. He agreed with me that the axle was bent. He turned to me and said 'Well done, lad. It's a bent axle. You'll get a fiver and a day's holiday for spotting that.'

"A day or so later I was called to the Area Manager's Office.

Radyr pilot No.09 015 crossing the viaduct over the River Taff on a trip working to Cathays, via the Llandaff Loop. (R. H. Marrows)

I was shown a letter from Mr E. R. Williams, Divisional Manager, British Railways (Western Region), thanking me for my vigilance as the wagon with the bent axle would have caused problems — or even an accident — had it been included in the coal train for Scunthorpe. I did receive a commendation for that which I never saw but it was put on my record. And despite what the examiner had told me, I did not receive a fiver and a day's holiday!

"The commendation made me feel rather pleased with myself and I must have thought that I was flavour of the month. I was about to leave the office when the Area Manager stopped me. His mood had suddenly changed and I wondered why. 'While you're here, Morris, I've been looking at your sick record. During the past six months you've had two days off, both of them Mondays. Don't let it happen again. I'll be keeping an eye on you.' I had never felt so deflated in my life. I had entered the man's office feeling very satisfied and full of myself, but came out with my tail between my legs. Although sometimes remote, top management never missed a trick.

"In 1974 a vacancy came up for under shunter which is really a second man to the head shunter. I got the job thinking that one day I would be head shunter and two years later I *did*

become head shunter. This meant an extra £5 a week which was useful as that was the year I got married.

"I sometimes came across men who were moaners by nature. They were never happy unless they were moaning. One such man was a shunter at Penarth North Curve. It was his custom to ring us up each morning to enquire as to how many wagons we had for him, then when he was informed he would always, without fail, complain that he had no room for them. An 08 Class 0-6-0 did a trip with about eight tank wagons to North Curve and the driver, when he returned to Radyr, reported to us that the man's siding was empty! The man just loved moaning.

"Some members of the public have a funny idea about railways and I encountered one in a pub in Radyr. We had been busy as usual one afternoon so we decided to take refreshments in the pub when the shift finished. We were in the bar enjoying a quiet drink. There was a man next to me who spoke to me and it was nothing more than small talk.

During the course of our conversation he asked me what I did for a living. I told him I was a shunter down in the yard. At this he became rather off-hand and haughty and stated that I was responsible for keeping him awake all night owing to the clanking wagons. But I think I had the answer. I asked him how long he had lived in Radyr, to which he replied three years. I was quick off the mark and reminded him that trains had been running through Radyr since 1840 and by that I didn't mean twenty minutes to seven! That was the end of our brief conversation.

"In 1982, when the Pope visited Cardiff, a lot of excursions were run to bring people to hear him speak. They came from Liverpool, London and many other places for the day. Following arrival at Cardiff, these excursions worked empty stock up to Radyr and the trains were stabled for the best part of the day near Radyr Quarry and on the up relief between Radyr and Walnut Tree. There were nine trains stabled there and on arrival the engines uncoupled and ran off to Canton for servicing. They returned in the evening to pick up their trains which meant they ran down the up relief until they reached the junction at Radyr.

"The Llandaff Loop was used only for traffic exiting the yard and travelling down the main line to Cardiff to run westward. Traffic bound for London, Scunthorpe and other places to the east left the yard via Radyr Quarry running along the branch which, with the introduction of the passenger service from Cardiff to Radyr via Ninian Park and Danescourt, become known as the City Line.

"The miners' strike of 1984/85 had a profound effect on the fortunes of Radyr yard. It appeared to me that this was the beginning of the end. The traffic dropped alarmingly. Merry-go-round trains had started some time earlier which robbed us of work although taking a load of coal from a colliery direct to Aberthaw power station made sense. During the miners' strike we were allowed to send one train up to the Nantgarw Coke Ovens on condition that it was accompanied by a letter jointly signed by officials of the Rail Union and the Miners' Union. This was done in order to clear the way and keep the pickets happy.

"I do not exaggerate when I say that I can remember trainloads of coal in hopper wagons standing idle in Radyr yard. They had been there so long that the sulphur in the coal caused corrosion in the base of the hoppers. In fact coal began to spill out underneath and they appeared, in wintertime, like yellow icicles hanging below the wagons.

"By 1988 there was little work at Radyr and the future looked bleak. There were some shifts where I had nothing to do. I had hoped that one day I would be the supervisor able to pass on my knowledge of yard work to the younger generation as at that time the supervisors were getting on in years. But it wasn't to be. With a feeling of regret I decided to look to the future and move on as I had a wife, two daughters and a mortgage. Overtime had disappeared so I, along with a friend, a fellow shunter, looked through the vacancy list.

"My colleague — I'll call him K .— was also eager to move as he had family commitments. He was a good chap and conscientious and it is not a word of a lie that he would arrive at work clean-shaven. By the end of the shift he had a beard! It was amazing, but he could grow a beard in one shift! Perhaps that is why I have always remembered him.

"We consulted the vacancy list and there were two jobs that appealed. One was for a signalman at Black Lion, between Abercynon and Merthyr. This was what was known as an exhausted vacancy, one which they had trouble filling. They couldn't get anyone to go there. The other vacancy was for a foreman at Tidal Sidings at Cardiff. K. was a valleys man and I knew he wanted the Tidal job. Owing to my seniority I got first choice of job. He was relieved when I told him that I would apply for signalman at Black Lion.

"I got the job at Black Lion. I was pleased at this as I lived in Merthyr Vale. I could roll out of bed in the morning and within two minutes I could be on duty in the box. There was no travelling involved. K. got the job at Tidal and he was happy. He had no transport so he bought himself a little moped to get himself to his place of work. But he didn't last long in the job; a few days after I had left Radyr I learned that K. was killed on his way to work, leaving a pregnant wife and four young daughters. So you can see that my memories of Radyr are bitter-sweet. The yard lingered on for about five years after I left and finally closed in March 1993."

Thus ended Joel Morris' adventures at Radyr Junction. He moved on to Black Lion where he learned the secrets of signalling, eventually progressing to Abercynon and to several other boxes where he acted as relief signalman.

In 2002, fourteen years after Mr. Morris' career as a shunter at Radyr ended, he returned there in his capacity as a mobile operations manager. In my final interview with him he had this to say about Radyr:

"The yard was always full of wagons and it was unusual to see an empty siding anywhere. Now, in my capacity as a manager, I am required to visit Radyr yard to investigate cases of trespass and vandalism and to make sure trains run safely. I stand in the yard and there are trees five feet tall in places. Sometimes I come across reminders of those far-off days: a discarded vacuum pipe or an old corrugated cabin. There are times when I think I can hear the voices of old workmates forming yet another train. I can imagine the diesel shunter racing around the place. We were always busy and it was hard work especially in winter when there was ice, snow, wind and rain. Except for that sad event I mentioned earlier I generally have fond memories of Radyr Junction."

8

Railway Rambles

A peep into the past

Walking abandoned railways is a harmless and satisfying pastime. I have done this many times alone or occasionally in the company of members of the Bristol Railway Circle. This organisation of railway enthusiasts was founded in 1934 and since 1968 has organised a 'Welsh Walk' on or as near to 1st March, St. David's Day,

each year. Some of the walks on which I have accompanied the Bristol Railway Circle will be recalled during the narrative which follows.

An abandoned railway can, at times, be a walk down memory lane. And when one ambles over the grass-covered ballast of a line over which one formerly travelled, memories

Photographs of motive power on the TVR's Nelson branch are particularly rare. This example was 'rescued' using modern techniques and is taken from a small contact print that was in poor condition. In this view of the three-arched masonry bridge which carried the branch over Mafon Road (formerly Sir Christopher Smith's tram road), a Pontypridd—Nelson train has just left Llanfabon Road Halt and is heading for the Nelson terminus. The locomotive is a former TVR '04' Class 0-6-2T which had been fitted with a GWR boiler. The exact date of the photograph is not known but is believed to be around 1930, about two years before the passenger service was withdrawn from the branch on 12th September 1932. (Author's Collection)

are stirred recalling happier times. It can also be an odd experience as on occasions one's memory can play strange tricks: Was the platform really that long? I'm certain the signal box stood there, or was it further along? That post was the down fixed distant! No it wasn't, it was the advanced starter. A foreman platelayer lived in that house. No, he didn't, but a lineman did!

On some lines it pays to use one's imagination. The former Taff Vale Railway branch from Pontypridd to Nelson is a good example of an abandoned line where imagination must be used. This unlucky line closed in 1932, thirteen years before I was born. I therefore have no memory of its day-to-day operation. Photographs of traffic at work on the branch are rare and in 40 years of searching for pictorial evidence I have managed to unearth only two such examples. The first artefact I discovered was a milepost at the rear of Blaen Nant House, Nelson, in the 1950s. I kept my eye on it for future recovery. Alas, someone got there before me.

Much of the lower end of the Nelson branch has been lost following the construction of the A470 trunk road. Station remains at Cilfynydd were swept away. Pont Shon Norton viaduct can still be seen and serves a useful purpose by carrying a service pipeline over the River Taff.

North of Traveller's Rest, much of the trackbed of the Nelson branch is intact. The first feature one encounters is the inclined plane on the original Llancaiach branch which dates back to 1841. The rope-worked incline, which had a gradient of 1 in 11, was later abandoned in favour of a locomotive

A postcard view of the TVR station at Nelson. The exact date is not known but is probably around 1910. The station nameboard can be seen beneath the far end of the canopy. Note the slope leading up to the junction of Commercial Street and Dynevor Terrace. Nelson Goods was on the far side of the road overbridge. Locomotive-hauled passenger trains were required to draw forward to the goods yard where there was a loop which allowed the engine to run round its train. The site of the station was filled in by 1957 and became a flower garden, lawn and, a short distance behind the photographer, a bus station. Almost a century after this photograph was taken there has been much change with the exception of the chimney-potted 'roofline' which appears very much the same today. (Author' Collection)

deviation which met the original branch a mile or so further north at St. Cynon's.

From the head of the incline to the site of Llanfabon Road Halt, on the outskirts of Nelson, is a pleasant walk of about two miles. The gradient along the way for the walker is easy and from the alignment there are panoramic views of the Taff and Aberdare valleys. There were two bridges at Bont-y-Ffrwd. One, on the later deviation, carried a road over the line to White Hall Golf Club. The bridge survived for 40 years but was demolished when the approach cutting was filled-in during the early 1970s. The other, which carried the original branch over a cattle creep, was demolished by way of an exercise in the use of explosives by the Home Guard during the Second World War.

At St. Cynon's, which overlooks Fiddler's Elbow and a fast-flowing weir on the River Taff, the original line and deviation met. It is at this location that one's imagination needs to be used. As one looks back down the branch towards Traveller's Rest, the 1 in 40 rising gradient is apparent. In the early part of the twentieth century TVR railmotors struggled for adhesion on this stretch and must have wheezed a sigh of relief when the sharp curve to an easier gradient was reached. Spectacular, too, must have been the sight of a heavy Llanharry—Dowlais iron ore train as it squealed around the curve at Fiddler's Quarry.

A few chains north, the Nelson branch left the valley of the Taff by swinging sharply to the east before passing through pleasantly-wooded Cwm Mafon. The leisurely, rural walk along the Nelson branch ends near the site of Llanfabon Road Halt. A stone's throw away, the Railway Inn serves as a reminder that one of Nelson's four stations once stood on the nearby embankment to serve the settlements of Abernant and Tai'r Heol. (I should make it clear here that not all four stations were open for public use at one and the same time.)

The site of the timber-built halt is marked by a grassy mound of earth and ballast. There is a nice little story concerning the halt which was related to me many years ago by the daughter of the man who lit the platform's oil lamp each day. The loyal old gentleman was Mr. Henry Brace who was paid a retainer

The abandoned TVR terminus at Nelson, looking towards Pontypridd c1951. Following closure in 1932, the building was put to a number of uses. First it was a GWR Railwaymen's Institute and finally it served as an ironmonger's storeroom. Telegraph poles mark the alignment of the single line branch. In the distance it curved through a cutting and passed to the right of Blean Nant House in the background. Beyond the house by a few hundred yards was the site of Berthgron Siding. (Author's Collection)

Long after the closure and abandonment of the TVR Nelson branch, this road overbridge at Bont-y-Ffrwd, near Traveller's Rest, survived carrying an access road to the Whitehall Golf Club and to Llanfabon. The cutting which the bridge crossed was filled-in in the 1970s and the parapets removed. Up until this time British Railways (Western Region) still displayed a metal notice nearby warning the public not to dump rubbish on their property! The village of Treharris can be seen through the arch. (Glyn E. Richards)

by the TVR and GWR companies for lighting the lamp during the hours of darkness year in and year out. It was the responsibility of the guard of the last train to extinguish the lamp. For performing his duty, Mr. Brace was paid one shilling (5p) a year!

Half a mile to the east, the Nelson terminus has disappeared without trace except for the iron parapet of a road overbridge in the village centre. Over 70 years have passed since the passenger service was withdrawn and one would have to be an octogenarian to have memories of the station and the trains that puffed in from Pontypridd.

In the early days of the branch, Nelson was provided with a signal box which stood at the north end of the station, between the road overbridge and the goods yard. By 1907 the signal box was closed and the electric train staff instrument housed in the station building. A key on the staff unlocked the goods yard ground frame. The other staff stations on the branch were at Pont Shon Norton and Cilfynydd Loop.

In 1930 there were plans to run the branch service through to Nelson & Llancaiach, so that some kind of connecting service could be provided with the Vale of Neath and the branch to Dowlais. The plan was shelved, however, no doubt because the writing was on the wall for the Nelson branch. In its early days it appears to have just about paid its way, but with competition from private and local authority omnibus services, the branch stood little chance of survival. It is easy to understand why the branch failed: other than Pontypridd, there

The lower end of the ex-TVR Nelson branch remained in use until the early 1970s to serve Albion Colliery, Cilfynydd. On 11th July 1959 a DMU on a Stephenson Locomotive Society special has come to a stand north of the colliery. The line in the foreground originally continued to Traveller's Rest and Nelson until withdrawal of the passenger service in 1932. The metals from Nelson back to Cilfynydd were lifted around 1936 and that which remained and is shown here — the north inlet — was used as a headshunt for pushing empties into the colliery yard. Loaded wagons left the yard via the south inlet. The Pont Shon Norton Junction signalman was responsible for traffic to Albion Colliery off the ex-TVR main line. The colliery closed in 1970 and once all coal stocks had been removed, the line was finally closed and the signal box taken out of use. (Ian L. Wright)

there were only two stops on the branch at its southern end and these were at Berw Road and Coedpenmaen, the latter being an early closure in 1922. North of Cilfynydd there was hardly any population to speak of until Nelson was reached. The local buses won the day simply because they could stop at almost every street corner.

The branch closed in 1932 but the station building at Nelson stood for another twenty years. It was put to various uses. At first it was used as a GWR Railwayman's Institute and finally as an ironmonger's warehouse. The building was demolished in the early 1950s and by 1957 the site was filled in. A flower garden, lawn and bus station now occupy the site of Nelson TVR. For the final timetable see Appendix.

Standing in the disused cutting at the eastern portal of Quaker's Yard West Tunnel has often caused my memory to play tricks. This tunnel, unventilated and of tight clearance, was on the single line tokenless section between Quaker's Yard (High Level) and Quaker's Yard West Tunnel box on the Vale of Neath line. At times it rejoiced under a number of names: Duffryn Tunnel, Quaker's Yard Tunnel and Cefn Glas Tunnel, but railwaymen generally referred to it as West Tunnel.

After the Second World War when there was no Sunday service the first train of the day on Mondays during winter had to approach the eastern portal with caution purely for the safety of the footplatemen. The portal was permanently damp and during winter weekends icicles formed and hung menacingly from the arch of the portal. Water running off

A postcard view of two of the viaducts at Quaker's Yard. In this view, looking north towards Merthyr, single line Vale of Neath is the nearest, with Joint Line viaduct immediately behind. Both structures are shown supported by stout timber frameworks. The Merthyr tram road ran beneath both viaducts and its alignment can be seen on the extreme right. (Author's Collection)

Cefn Glass mountain gathered above the tunnel mouth. In fact the dried-up cut of the Glamorganshire Canal passed above and within a few feet of the portal. It required the first train of the day to dislodge the icicles in as gentle a manner as possible otherwise driver and fireman might have suffered serious injuries had some of the frozen spears found their way into the cab.

I have mentioned elsewhere in this book that there was a considerable variety of motive power working along the Vale of Neath. Its twisting cross-valley route apart, the locomotives large and small working freight and passenger traffic made it the most interesting of through routes and one could never be sure what class of engine would be at the head of a train.

It is when I have stood in the cutting looking at the eastern portal of West Tunnel that I have had to scratch my head and ask myself the question: Did 'Grange' and 'Castle' 4-6-0s actually squeeze into the tunnel, let alone '57XX' Class 0-6-0PTs and '56XX' Class 0-6-2Ts? Forty years after the tunnel ceased to be used the cutting and portal can still be seen from the A470 trunk road.

Five miles away to the east is Hengoed on the ex-Rhymney Railway main line. There were two stations here, Low Level and High Level, the latter on the Pontypool Road—Neath line. Low Level survives today as plain Hengoed and is nothing more than a basic station with bus-shelter accommodation. It is well-patronised by those commuting daily to work in Caerphilly and Cardiff. When both stations were in use they were linked by a system of subways, steps and ramps and the administration of both stations was conducted at Low Level.

High Level was abandoned in 1964. I remember the station with mixed feelings as it was here that I, as an unwilling schoolboy, changed trains with about 60 willing scholars, when travelling to school at Caerphilly in the 1950s.

Hengoed viaduct was the destination for the 2003 Welsh Walk of the Bristol Railway Circle in which I participated. I had not seen the station in abandoned state for 30 years but was surprised to discover that both platforms were still intact even though 30ft high birch trees had grown on the very spots where I had stood waiting for a train 45 years earlier.

The station stood on a cramped site, the down platform being perched precariously on the edge of a fearsomely steep drop of about 100ft down to the main Rhymney Valley highway. The buildings have long since been demolished. The waiting room on the down platform was constructed in cantilever fashion out over the precarious drop. The building may have disappeared, but the two stout rusting iron girders, which for decades kept the building suspended in mid-air, survive.

Revisiting Hengoed (High Level) in 2003 was an odd experience for me and likewise for one of my Bristol colleagues in particular. We must have been thinking along the same lines but he was first to ask the question: "Did trains actually run through this station? There doesn't seem enough width between the platforms!"

But in a way traffic *still* passes through Hengoed (High Level). This takes the form of energetic cyclists and brisk walkers using the recently-established cycle track which has been laid through the station and over Hengoed viaduct. Expensive mountain bikes have replaced pannier tanks and walkers in air-cushioned trainers have replaced gangers in hob-nailed boots.

One of the saddest sights in south east Wales is isolated Cwmbargoed on the exposed Dowlais Moors. Today it is a railhead for coal-loading and occasional stone trains although during the past few years it has seen little use. The mountain

community of Cwmbargoed has its roots in coalmining. In the early nineteenth century a number of balance pits was sunk in the area providing work for hundreds of people.

However, it was the opening in 1876 of the Taff Bargoed Joint Railway that enabled Cwmbargoed to develop into what can be reasonably described as a railway village. It was one of two original intermediate stations on the line, the other being at Bedlinog. Trelewis Platform was a later addition, being brought into use in 1911.

Cwmbargoed grew in importance when the Dowlais Iron Company laid sidings on the mountain-top alongside the joint line. As there had been insufficient land available at the works the next best location was Cwmbargoed. It wasn't a village in the accepted sense but a scattered community. It had no shops and most household supplies were delivered by railway. Costermongers called regularly, travelling over rough mountain tracks from the steeltown of Dowlais, a couple of miles distant. Most of the dwellings huddled around the railway and there were two rows of houses; these were known as Railway Terrace and Pit Row.

Cwmbargoed's spiritual needs were provided by the Railway Mission and religious meetings, which were inter-denominational, were held in a building created by the cannibalisation of two signal boxes. The Cwmbargoed Railway Mission, when established, was one of only two in Wales, the other being at Builth Wells.

The biggest enemy of the railwayman and inhabitants of Cwmbargoed was the weather. While it was early spring in the

A prominent feature of the railway complex at Quaker's Yard was the extensive metal footbridge which connected High Level and Low Level stations. In this view taken on 26th September 1960, pupils of the local grammar school use the footbridge to reach the up platform of Low Level station for their homeward journey. Ex-GWR '56XX' Class 0-6-2T No.5677, of Merthyr shed (88D), waits at the platform with the 3.47pm Pontypridd—Merthyr school train. The line to the right is the up refuge siding. On the extreme left can be seen the Quaker's Yard branch which connected the ex-Taff Vale main line with the Vale of Neath. (HCC/RMC)

25 years after abandonment, the eastern portal of Quaker's Yard tunnel is waterlogged and mother nature has had her way. Note the small amount of terra firma above the tunnel mouth. This was necessary when the tunnel was bored through Cefn Glas, as the cut of the Glamorganshire Canal passed within a few yards of the portal. It is an odd experience (or an illusion) these days to stand at the entrance to the tunnel as it does not look wide or high enough to accommodate even an 0-6-0PT. (Author)

sheltered valleys, it was still winter at Cwmbargoed. This was hardly surprising as it stood in a slight depression on the Dowlais Moors, 1,250ft above sea level. It is therefore little wonder that the Cwmbargoed-born author, historian and weatherman Mr. Josh Powell, in describing life in the railway village, decided to name his self-published book *Living in the Clouds.*

The summit of the joint line was a few chains west of Cwmbargoed signal box. One of the biggest problems was snow piling up in the long, deep cutting which ran towards Penydarren Pits Platform. Such were the conditions in this cutting that it was necessary to run a pair of pannier tanks, coupled bunker to bunker, both fitted with a snowplough, up and down the cutting to keep it clear during falling snow.

Lampman Mr. L. M. Whiteman, whose working life is touched on elsewhere in this book, worked at Cwmbargoed in late 1964. He described it as being "an overcoat colder than anywhere else I had worked". Cwmbargoed was not only a difficult place for railwaymen to carry out their work. The inhabitants of the village were equally hardy souls and had to endure atrocious conditions. The bitter winters of 1947 and 1963 tested everyone and for weeks on end the village was snowbound but the railway provided a vital lifeline. Houses and cottages at Cwmbargoed were illuminated by oil lamps; the village did not receive an electricity supply until 1958.

The rear of the main station building at Cwmbargoed stood at right angles to the head of the Taff Bargoed Valley. From its rear window it was possible to see a Cae Harris '56XX' Class

Hengoed viaduct, 23rd July 1962. In this view looking east towards Maesycwmmer Junction, ex-GWR '56XX' 0-6-2T No.6697 is approaching Hengoed (High Level) with a Pontypool Road—Neath train. The B&M Brecon—Newport line can be seen emerging from the furthest arch at the end of the viaduct. (E. V. Richards)

0-6-2T labouring with two carriages up the steep gradient just after it had left Bedlinog, 3 miles and 33 chains to the south. For this heavily-graded stretch between the two stations, thirteen minutes were allowed for the up journey; eight minutes only were required in the down direction.

The station had the services of a station master up until the 1930s. However, it was the withdrawal of the passenger service between Nelson & Llancaiach and Dowlais (Cae Harris) in June 1964 that brought about the biggest change of all. The loss of the trains was a body blow to the good people of the old railway village. A replacement bus service to Dowlais was provided but proved something of a failure. By

1965 most of the inhabitants had moved away to Dowlais and Merthyr Tydfil. The Railway Mission closed and the close-knit mountain community at Cwmbargoed died.

A few years ago I drove to Cwmbargoed, parked my car and wandered around what was left of the village. I was informed by the chargeman, who occupied a Portakabin next to the sidings, that not a soul lived there any more. Railway Terrace and Pit Row had long since been demolished but on the site of the station traces of the up platform were visible.

As far as Cwmbargoed is concerned, it has been a case of 'all change'. On second thoughts, this is not quite true. The only things that have not changed are the wild, windswept moorland scenery — and the weather!

At Dowlais, 2½ miles away — or a mile and half as the crow flies — the Cae Harris terminus of the Taff Bargoed Joint, was swept away many years ago. It was the last of Dowlais' stations to provide a public passenger service. The modest terminus had one arrival/departure platform and a short bay. The station was a fine example of the Rhymney Railway's architectural style and could reasonably be described as having an ecclesiastical appearance. The passenger service between Cae Harris and Nelson & Llancaiach, which showed

81

The up platform at Cwmbargoed as seen from a Dowlais (Cae Harris)—Nelson & Llancaiach train on 10th July 1958. For almost 90 years the station building, which stood at right angles to the Taff Bargoed valley, took the full force of the vicious weather experienced at Cwmbargoed. Beyond the signal box is the summit of the line and also visible are the houses which were known as Railway Terrace. Of interest in this view is the double slip at the end of the platform and the Rhymney Railway signal just beyond the station building. The gradient through the station was steep and this feature is highlighted by the station nameboard which is level – compare it with the platform edge. (HCC/RMC)

---

little variation throughout the line's history, consisted of four or five trains either way on weekdays with a number of extras on Saturdays. And there were oddities, too. For instance, in early 1958, there was a turn, part of the K1 sixteen-hour duty when, on Saturdays only, a train ran empty coaching stock from Dowlais to Bedlinog. After hanging about at the hillside village for about for ten minutes it then formed the 1.35pm Bedlinog to Nelson and the return 1.56pm Nelson—Dowlais. One can only wonder why it worked ecs to Bedlinog, leaving out Cwmbargoed.

A few hundred yards south of the Dowlais terminus stood Dowlais (Cae Harris) depot, which was a sub-shed to Merthyr (88D). This was a three-road shed opened in 1876. A turntable was provided at the rear. In the final years four of the ex-GWR '56XX' class 0-6-2Ts were sufficient to manage the line's passenger and freight traffic. The shed closed to steam in December 1964 after which, without its roof, it was used for a few years as a stabling point for the new Type 3 (Class 37) diesel locomotives.

In 1984 the single freight-only line between Dowlais and Cwmbargoed was lifted following the closure of the Ivor Works. Thus ended the old steeltown's affair with the iron road. The town was once served by seven railway stopping places: these were at Cae Harris (GWR/RR), High Street (LNWR), Pant, Dowlais Top and Central (Brecon & Merthyr) and two halts at Pantyscallog (Low Level on the LNWR line and High Level on the B&M branch to Central).

Back at Quaker's Yard, even today a railway ramble will pay dividends to the historian. Since the late 1960s much of what was an extensive railway complex has been swept away. Where once there were two stations, a branch connecting the Vale of Neath with the ex-Taff Vale main line, a tunnel which I have already mentioned, and three viaducts, all that remains in practical railway terms is a single line running through the former down platform of Low Level station.

Fortunately, a fine band of photographers have preserved Quaker's Yard as it was in busier times on film. It is their black and white images in books and albums which remind me that today Quaker's Yard is truly a forgotten junction. Following the closure in 1964, High Level station was demolished and virtually all trace of it has been removed. A private housing estate now occupies the site together with the trackbed of the branch from Low Level to Quaker's Yard East Junction. However, there are two features that survive to remind one that there was actually a station known as Quaker's Yard (High Level). The first is a flight of stone steps alongside a retaining wall which led from the village of Edwardsville to the station. The second is the Great Western Hotel, a small hostelry which benignly overlooks the site.

In 1971 the ex-Taff Vale line from Abercynon to Merthyr was singled with a passing place provided at Black Lion, thus only the former down platform at Low Level was retained for passenger use. The station building, of Taff Vale origin, was demolished, replaced by a characterless waiting shelter.

Quaker's Yard had three viaducts which added much interest to the general scene. The first to be built was Taff Vale, on the Cardiff—Merthyr line, which carried its first traffic in 1841. The second was Vale of Neath (or Number One viaduct) on the Pontypool—Neath line which was brought into use in about 1864. The third was Joint Line viaduct (Number Two) completed in 1886. This carried the Quaker's Yard & Merthyr Joint line from High Level over the River Taff to the western flank of the valley.

Today, Taff Vale viaduct alone survives. Its task nowadays is comparatively easy when one considers the heavy traffic that once tested its strength. Only two-car Sprinters and Pacers cause its masonry muscles to be flexed these days. From 1918 all three viaducts were supported by stout timber frameworks placed inside the arches which had the effect of making them

Looking towards the stopblocks at Dowlais (Cae Harris), terminus of the Taff Bargoed Joint on 10th July 1958. Ex-GWR '56XX' Class 0-6-2T No.5630 stands at the platform with the 4.15p.m. to Ystrad Mynach. There was no engine release at this station and following arrival at the platform, a train had to be pushed back towards Dowlais shed for the run-round procedure to be carried out, following which a train was propelled back to the platform. In later days the bay platform to the right was used to stable coaches. (HCC/RMC)

83

appear worryingly unsafe. The reason for this was mining subsidence. The timber providing support for Taff Vale viaduct was removed in 1955, but the two others remained supported until long after abandonment of their respective lines.

Joint Line viaduct suffered most from the effects of subsidence and it is interesting here to relate how the structure was finally considered unsafe and subsequently closed to traffic. Ganger W. J. Rogers of Treharris, in the course of his duties, made the alarming discovery of a 45ft crack in the viaduct. He reported his findings immediately to his superiors and traffic was stopped. When the ballast was removed, investigation revealed an eighteen-inch hole over the second

---

Cae Harris shed, 10th July 1958, with two members of the '56XX' Class near the original timber-built coaling stage. Its replacement, the unattractive corrugated iron clad building in the centre of the picture was brought into use some time in 1957. A turntable — little used in the final years — was situated to the rear of the three-road shed. The Taff Bargoed line ran between the wooden coaling stage and the shed. Cae Harris station is about one hundred yards out of shot to the left. Note the waste heaps in the background and a heavily-laden lorry travelling down the locally famous 'slip road' which linked Dowlais Top with Pentrebach. (HCC/RMC)

arch of the eight-span bridge. A crack was also discovered running from one parapet to the other. The viaduct was never again used after that discovery was made on a cold morning early in 1951.

Both viaducts were demolished by explosion in 1969 and inquisitive crowds turned out to witness the noisy event. A ramble along the Merthyr Tram Road, perhaps better known as the Penydarren Tram Road on which Trevithick ran his locomotive in 1804 for a bet, will afford views of the eastern abutments of the two viaducts. And there is a bonus on the tram road, which is now part of the Taff Trail, for here and there are reminders of Trevithick's famous excursion in the form of stone blocks which acted as sleepers. The surviving Taff Vale viaduct has features of interest as it was originally built to carry a single line but was widened in 1862. Thus two viaducts glued together with stone and mortar took shape. Brunel's earlier more ornate design is to the west.

On a melancholy afternoon in November 1966 I found myself at Aberfan and decided to walk south along the abandoned trackbed of the Quaker's Yard & Merthyr Joint line as far as Joint Line viaduct, a distance of about 1¾ miles. This line had been opened by the GWR and Rhymney Railway in 1886. At Merthyr Vale Junction a branch crossed the River Taff by way of a viaduct to reach Nixon's Colliery at Merthyr Vale. As I mentioned earlier, owing to the condition of Joint Line viaduct the lower end of the line closed suddenly in 1951. The remainder of the line to Merthyr was closed in stages.

An undated postcard view of Bedlinog station during the Rhymney Railway period. The gradient through the station was 1 in 54 rising towards Cwmbargoed. The station buildings were a fine example of the Rhymney Railway's architectural style. Nothing remains of the station today except for the single line to Cwmbargoed. (Author's Collection)

At the time of my first and only walk along this line, I knew very little of its history. As I neared the viaduct I came across what appeared to be platform remains next to a minor road overbridge. Above the line stood a row of terraced houses. Later, with the aid of a little research and a map, I discovered that there had been a stopping place there to serve what was a remote, sparsely-populated byway. I had stumbled across the site of Pontygwaith Halt which was opened by the GWR on 11th September 1933. The platforms, I guessed, had been built of timber and a path from both led up to the overbridge. There was a railway cottage nearby which was once the home of a platelayer.

The Joint Line between Quaker's Yard and Merthyr received little attention from the photographers who were active in South Wales in the 1950s. Its sudden closure seemed to catch many of them napping, added to which the withdrawal of the passenger service occurred during the time of a fuel crisis.

Railway access apart, Pontygwaith was what most people would have considered to be off the beaten track. Few, if any, photographs appear to exist of the halt. I have never seen even the crudest snapshot of the place. For me and for the time being, Pontygwaith Halt and the way in which it appeared, remains a mystery.

The last occasion on which I boarded a train at Pontypool Road was in the summer of 1963. I have many memories of the big island platform and canopy at Pontypool Road and the booking office at the end of the gloomy subway at road level. My earliest memories of the station are hazy to say the least, but I can distinctly remember an ex-GWR diesel railcar stabled in the north bay. I changed trains at Pontypool Road when returning from West Country holidays and whilst adults grumbled about the interminable wait for a Vale of Neath connection, I enjoyed hanging about watching the north to west, and vice-versa, trains in and out of the station. While I spent a pleasant hour watching with interest, the adults passed an hour drinking stewed Western Region tea in the station's refreshment room.

I mentioned in the introduction that events passed me by during the changes, upheavals and rationalisations of the early to mid-1960s. This was also true of Pontypool Road. I had completely forgotten about the place.

It was by chance that in 1971 a railway employee with inside knowledge informed me that the ban on steam had been lifted and that privately-owned or preserved locomotives would be allowed to run once again on the metals of British Railways.

*The King and his loyal subjects! In 1972 large crowds of
people, young and old and boys of all ages, turned out
to see ex-GWR 'King' Class 4-6-0 No.6000*
King George V *at Pontypool Road. On this occasion
the the engine was en route to Hereford with the
Bulmer's Cider train.* (Author's Collection)

RIGHT:
*In 1971 numbered souvenir tickets were issued
as platform tickets to view* King George V
*when the locomotive was on tour with the
Bulmer's special train. The ticket was
purchased at Newport and the price
was 5p*
(Author's Collection)

ADMIT ONE

SOUVENIR TICKET

to view the Great Western Railway
locomotive no. 6000 'King George V'
on tour with H. P. Bulmer Ltd
special train 2 to 9 October 1971.

Total weight 137 tons 4 cwt. in working order.
Length 68 feet 2 inches.
Tractive effort 39,000 lb.
Driving wheels 6 feet 6 inches
Bogie wheels 3 feet.

Water capacity 4000 gallons.
Coal capacity 6 tons.
Boiler pressure 250 lb. square inch.
Cylinders (4) 16 inches × 28 inches.

No .. 1017

The insider provided me with the timings for the first run to be
undertaken under the new conditions when ex-GWR 'King'
Class 4-6-0 No.6000 *King George V* would head a train of
Pullman cars from Hereford to Birmingham and would pass
through Pontypool Road.

This was an opportunity not to be missed. Here was the
chance not only to see the GWR flagship in action, but a
chance to have another look at Pontypool Road after a break
of eight years.

My first reaction was one of disbelief when I, accompanied
by my wife and a friend, turned left into the road that led down
to the station. The old booking office was still in place, but
above the subway steps the platform, except for a shelter, was
bare. The buildings and canopy had gone. The north and south

During the 1970s No.6000 King George V *made regular appearances between Newport and Hereford. In this 1972 photograph, the locomotive has just re-started the H. P. Bulmer Ltd. special train from Pontypool Road and is heading towards Little Mill en route to Hereford.* (Author)

bays were strewn with rubbish and weeds flourished between the flagstones. I had expected to see change but not as wholesale or as drastic as this. Pontypool Road had been reduced to the status of a glorified halt. It had become a blot on the landscape and served to highlight 'the couldn't care less' attitude that seemed to prevail at the time. The only features of interest were the remaining semaphore signals.

But I survived the shock and ten minutes later my spirits were raised. Around the curve from Little Mill appeared *King George V* with its rake of Pullman cars. The 'King' was in perfect condition as it ran, ticking like a watch, through the down platform. The locomotive with the bell had been polished to perfection, its copper-capped chimney and brass safety valve bonnet sparkled in the autumn sunshine and there was hardly a hint of exhaust. My view of the train was fleeting for, less than a minutes later, it passed beneath a road bridge and disappeared around the curve towards Panteg.

A fine array of signals on display at Pontypool Road, 11th July 1959. In this view looking north, ex-GWR 'Hall' Class 4-6-0 No.6903 Belmont Hall, *displaying express headcode, pulls into the down platform with the 11.45a.m. Manchester—Plymouth train. The north bay, once used by passenger traffic for the Monmouth line, can just be glimpsed behind the two figures in the distance.* (HCC/RMC)

I saw *King George V* at Pontypool Road several times in the years that followed, by which time such occasions were attracting enormous crowds. Everyone wanted to see the 'King' including fathers with sons who hitherto had never seen a steam locomotive in action. The 'King' was a star performer on the line during the 1970s. In 1972 the locomotive worked a train to Hereford but stopped at Pontypool Road much to the delight of the multitude of admirers who had turned out to have a closer look at Collett's masterpiece.

I had positioned myself by trespassing on the side of the line a hundred yards towards Little Mill in the hope of capturing on film a fiery restart from the platform. Not a bit of it. *King George V* pulled away with its train of ten Pullman cars with ease and with the minimum of fuss. Once again there was hardly a hint of exhaust, just the steady unmistakably loud bark of a GWR engine in first class fettle.

TRAFFIC OVER THE PENALLTAU BRANCH
Times shown are those at Penalltau Junction
(All B headcode except where shown)

Up Trains

	am
Rhymney-Taff Merthyr and Bedlinog workmen	5.37
(C) Coaches Rhymney-Bedlinog (SO)	6.04
(conveyed workmen from Ystrad Mynach)	
(K) Stonefield-Cwmbargoed freight	6.23
Ystrad Mynach-Neath (Riverside) passenger	7.23
	pm
Coaches Ystrad Mynach-Nelson (SX)	12/21
Aber Jct-Dowlais Cae Harris freight	12/28
Ystrad Mynach-Dowlais Cae Harris passenger (SO)	12/43
(K) Aber Jct-Dowlais Cae Harris freight	2/58
Bute Road-Quaker's Yard HL passenger (SX)	3/55
Cardiff (Queen Street)-Quaker's Yard HL passenger (SO)	3/55
Ystrad Mynach-Dowlais Cae Harris passenger	8/17
Ystrad Mynach-Dowlais Cae Harris passenger (SO)	10/10

Down Trains

	am
Aberdare (HL)-Ystrad Mynach passenger	6.52
Aberdare (HL)-Cardiff (Queen Street) passenger	8.37
(K) Cwmbargoed-Stonefield freight	9.45-9.50
(K) Dowlais Cae Harris-Aber Jct freight	10.30-10.35
	pm
Dowlais Cae Harris-Ystrad Mynach passenger	12/4
(C) Nelson-Rhymney coaches (SO)	12/32
(K) Dowlais Cae Harris-Aber Jct freight (SO)	1/07
(K) Dowlais Cae Harris-Aber Jct freight (SX)	1/20
Bedlinog-Rhymney workmen (SO)	1/52
Aberdare (HL)-Cardiff (Bute Road) passenger	2/04
Bedlinog-Rhymney workmen (SX)	3/19
Dowlais Cae Harris-Ystrad Mynach passenger	4/48
Dowlais Cae Harris-Ystrad Mynach passenger	7/16
Dowlais Cae Harris-Ystrad Mynach passenger	9/47

TRAFFIC THROUGH TORPANTAU
From the Working Time Book, January 1st 1895

Down

From	Time at Torpantau	Destination
	am	
Talyllyn (Night goods)	1.36	Pontsticill Junction
Brecon (goods, Mo, RR)	4.45	Rhydycar Junction
Brecon (Day goods)	6.50	Rhydycar Junction
Brecon (Brecon goods)	9.48	Pontsticill Junction
Brecon (Main line passenger)	8.31	Newport High Street
	pm	
Talyllyn (Day goods)	1.50	Merthyr, TV
Brecon (Main line passenger)	2.52	Newport High Street
Brecon (Merthyr branch passenger)	2.52	Merthyr, GW
(the above train runs coupled from Brecon to Pontsticill Junction)		
Brecon (Main line passenger)	5.48	Newport High Street
Talyllyn (Night goods)	7.15	Merthyr, TV

Up

From	Time at Torpantau	Destination
	am	
Pontsticill Junction (Night goods)	2.35	Talyllyn
Newport High Street (Main line passenger)	10.12	Brecon
Pontsicill Junction (Brecon goods)	10.32	Talyllyn
Pontsticill Junction (Goods, MO, RR)	11.25	Brecon
	pm	
Merthyr GW (Merthyr Branch goods)	12.45	Brecon
Newport High Street (Main line passenger)	3.10	Brecon
Merthyr GW (Day goods)	4.25	Talyllyn
Newport High Street (Main line passenger)	7.50	Brecon
Merthyr TV (Night goods)	10.45	Brecon
(MO, RR=Mondays only, runs as required)		

Mineral trains under Control Orders

Cardiff (Cathays Van Siding) to Rhymney Valley. C12 9.30am; C16 7.40am; C24 11.45am; C29 2/0pm; C31 4/20pm; C34 5/35; (RR Sats), C37 6/30pm (SX).
Barry (Cadoxton). B10 9.40am Taff Merthyr Colliery; B24 11.25am Rhymney Valley; B25 1/35pm Rhymney Valley; B30 3/5pm Taff Merthyr Colliery; B32 4/10pm Rhymney Valley (SX), Treharris (SO): B39 (SX) Taff Merthyr Colliery; B42 8/35 (SX) 6/35 (SO) Treharris.
Radyr Junction. Y23 12/10pm (SX) 11.10am (SO) Rhymney Valley.

ACKNOWLEDGEMENTS
I am indebted to the following individuals who were most helpful when there were many grey areas to be clarified: Mr. G. C. Andrews, Mr. R. J. Caston, Mr. N. Hadlow, Mr. R. Harman, Mrs. C. Jacob (Merthyr Tydfil Public Library), Mr. D. W. T. Jones (Bill Engine), Mr. R. H. Marrows, Mr. B. J. Miller, Mr J. V. Morris, Mr. R. Roper, Mr I. Thomas and Mr. L. M. Whiteman (ex-BR Western Region and a fount of local knowledge). Special thanks are extended to the railwaymen, named within, who took the trouble to enthusiastically relate to me recollections of their working lives. Thanks also to the photographers and copyright holders who gave permission for their work to be reproduced.